TOP 10
LOS ANGELES

CATHERINE GERBER

EYEWITNESS TRAVEL

Left **Sunset Strip** Right **Huntington Gardens**

LONDON, NEW YORK,
MELBOURNE, MUNICH AND DELHI
www.dk.com

Printed and bound by South China
Printing Co. Ltd, China
First published in Great Britain in 2004
by Dorling Kindersley Limited
80 Strand, London WC2R 0RL
A Penguin Company

14 15 16 17 10 9 8 7 6 5 4 3 2 1

Reprinted with revisions 2006, 2008,
2010, 2012, 2014
Copyright 2004, 2014
© Dorling Kindersley Limited, London
A Penguin Company

A CIP catalogue record is available from
the British Library.

ISBN 978 1 40932 640 3

Within each Top 10 list in this book, no
hierarchy of quality or popularity is implied.
All 10 are, in the editor's opinion, of roughly
equal merit.

Floors are referred to throughout in
accordance with British usage; ie the "first
floor" is the floor above ground level.

Contents

Los Angeles Top 10

The information in this DK Eyewitness Top 10 Travel Guide is checked regularly.
Every effort has been made to ensure that this book is as up-to-date as possible at the time of
going to press. Some details, however, such as telephone numbers, opening hours, prices,
gallery hanging arrangements and travel information are liable to change. The publishers
cannot accept responsibility for any consequences arising from the use of this book, nor for
any material on third party websites, and cannot guarantee that any website address in this
book will be a suitable source of travel information. We value the views and suggestions of
our readers very highly. Please write to: Publisher, DK Eyewitness Travel Guides,
Dorling Kindersley, 80 Strand, London, Great Britain WC2R 0RL, or email travelguides@dk.com.

Left **View of Downtown Los Angeles** Right *Homage to a Starry Night* mural, Venice Beach

Left **Redondo Beach** Right **Beverly Hills Hotel, Beverly Hills**

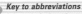

Key to abbreviations
Adm *admission charge* **Free** *no admission charge* **Dis. access** *disabled access*

3

LOS ANGELES
TOP 10

LOS ANGELES TOP 10

TOP 10 Los Angeles Highlights

The myth, the velocity, the edginess in creative and technological fields – this is Los Angeles, where the multicultural future that awaits the rest of the country is already a firm reality. In just over 200 years, LA has grown from a dusty Spanish outpost into one of the world's largest and most complex cities offering top venues for everything from archaeology and the arts to food. The birthplace of Mickey Mouse and Hollywood, LA has shaped the imaginations of millions.

1 Sunset Strip

The heady mix of hip restaurants, night-clubs, and bars along the city's entertainment mile attracts legions of the young and the trendy *(see pp8–9)*.

2 Historic Hollywood Boulevard

The boulevard that gave birth to the movie industry is still associated with the stars, even if the only ones around today are those embedded in the sidewalk *(see pp10–11)*.

3 The Getty Center

One of the best bargains in town, this striking hilltop complex is a marvel of modern architecture and a mecca for fans of European art. Stunning views *(see pp12–15)*.

4 Los Angeles County Museum of Art (LACMA)

One of the largest art museums in the US, LACMA offers a survey of artistic achievement in the world from prehistoric times to the present *(see pp16–19)*.

Previous pages **View of LA from Griffith Observatory**

5 El Pueblo de Los Angeles
This historic district preserves LA's oldest buildings, celebrating its Spanish-Mexican past with stores, eateries, and festivals (see pp20–21).

6 Huntington Library, Art Collections, & Botanical Gardens
One of LA's great cultural treasures invites visitors to experience its fine paintings, rare manuscripts, and gorgeous gardens (see pp22–5).

7 Universal Studios Hollywood℠
A day at Universal involves high-tech thrill rides, live action shows, and special effects extravaganzas. The Studio Tour takes visitors to the backlot of this actual working movie studio (see pp26–7).

8 Griffith Park
The largest city park in the nation offers a unique combination of rugged wilderness and such diversions as museums, a zoo, and an observatory. The landmark Hollywood Sign is located here as well (see pp28–9).

9 Disneyland® Resort
As timeless and ageless as Mickey Mouse himself, the original Disney park hasn't lost its magic over half a century after it first opened (see pp30–35).

10 Catalina Island
Catalina Island is a quick and easy getaway whose considerable charms include crystal-clear waters, miles of undeveloped backcountry, and a sense of being far away from the bustle of big city LA (see pp36–7).

⑩ Sunset Strip

Sunset Strip has been a haven of hedonism since Prohibition days. Wedged between Hollywood and Beverly Hills, this 1.7 miles (2.7 km) of the Sunset Boulevard is crammed with hot nightclubs, hip rock venues, and fashionable boutiques. During Hollywood's Glamour Age (1930–50), the stars trysted at the Chateau Marmont, partied at Trocadero, and talked shop at Schwab's Pharmacy. Today's hot spots rub shoulders with some historical landmarks.

Site of Schwab's Pharmacy
In the 1930s and 1940s, Schwab's Pharmacy was a hip hangout – Charlie Chaplin played pinball and James Dean sipped his coffee here. Torn down in 1988, the site is now occupied by a huge Virgin Megastore *(above)*.

The Strip by day

For fusion food at its finest, head to the über-trendy Asia de Cuba inside the Mondrian Hotel *(see p147)*.

Gaining entry to the trendiest venues is easiest around 9pm and on weeknights.

Avoid the traffic on the Strip on Friday and Saturday nights.

• Map L3
• Along Sunset Blvd between Crescent Heights Blvd & Doheny Dr
• Site of Schwab's Pharmacy: 8024 Sunset Blvd
• Sunset Strip Tattoo: 7524 W Sunset Blvd
• Sunset Plaza: 8600 & 8700 Sunset Blvd
• Andaz West Hollywood: 8401 Sunset Blvd
• Rainbow Bar & Grill: 9015 Sunset Blvd

Giant Billboards
A testimony to the Strip's unabashed commercialism, these mega-sized billboards promote movies, records, products, and individual stars, which is why they're also called "vanity boards" *(above)*.

Sunset Strip Tattoo
Julia Roberts got a Japanese symbol and Nicolas Cage a stingray at this tattoo studio to the stars that has also inked Ben Affleck and Pamela Anderson.

Sunset Strip by night

Chateau Marmont
Modeled on a French palace, this 1927 hotel *(below, p65, & p146)* has hosted celebrities such as Humphrey Bogart and Mick Jagger. Howard Hughes ogled at girls by the pool, and an overdosed John Belushi made his final dramatic exit in 1982.

5 Sunset Tower Hotel

This Art Deco gem *(above & p146)*, formerly known as the Argyle, opened in 1931 and has been the home of yesteryear stars. John Wayne allegedly kept a cow in the penthouse. Its bar is a hot address today.

9 Andaz West Hollywood

Formerly known as the "Riot Hyatt," this hotel tower is part of rock'n'roll history as party central for British bands in the 1960s and 1970s. Led Zeppelin cruised down the halls on motorcycles and Keith Richards mooned his fans.

10 Rainbow Bar & Grill

This rock'n'roll *boîte* fills with long-haired rockers and their hangers-on every night. When it was still the Villa Nova restaurant, Marilyn Monroe met Joe DiMaggio on a blind date, and John Belushi ate his final meal before overdosing on drugs.

Sunset Boulevard

Sunset Strip takes up only a small portion of the 25-mile (40-km) Sunset Boulevard. Following the path of an old Indian Trail, this major cross-town artery is a microcosm of the cultural, ethnic, and social cauldron that is LA. Starting at El Pueblo in Downtown, it travels west through different neighborhoods such as Silver Lake, Los Feliz, Hollywood, Beverly Hills, Bel Air, and Pacific Palisades, before spilling into the Pacific Ocean. Sunset Boulevard has played starring roles in the TV series *77 Sunset Strip* and the movie *Sunset Boulevard*.

6 Sunset Plaza

This two-block commercial stretch is lined with designer shops and Euro-style restaurants teeming with a hip crowd. Its appeal with celebrities such as Nicole Kidman and Cindy Crawford make it prime territory for star-searching *(below)*.

7 Viper Room

Actor River Phoenix died outside this club, once owned by Johnny Depp, in 1993. Few remember its earlier incarnation as the Melody Room, a favorite with Bugsy Siegel and his mobster pals *(see p64 & p106)*.

8 Whisky a Go-Go

A Strip fixture since 1963, the Whisky gave the world go-go dancing and the Doors, its house band in 1966. Other legends such as Jimi Hendrix and Janis Joplin also played here regularly. Today, new bands still get launched on occasion *(see p106)*.

Historic Hollywood Boulevard

Hollywood Boulevard, home of the Walk of Fame, has always been synonymous with the glamour of moviemaking, especially during its heydays in the 1920s and 1930s. But like an aging diva, it eventually fell out of favor, teeming with runaways, drug addicts, and prostitutes. Now the heart of Tinseltown is finally cleaning up its act – the old movie palaces have received facelifts, the mega-entertainment complex of Hollywood and Highland is a major draw, and even "Oscar" has found a permanent home here.

Hand- and footprints in TCL Chinese Theatre

○ For addictive cream puffs, head for Beard Papa's inside the Hollywood and Highland complex.

○ Red signs along the boulevard indicate places the stars used to hang out in.

The visitors center at the Hollywood and Highland is open 10am–10pm Mon–Sat, 10am–7pm Sun.

• Map P2
• Stretches from La Brea Blvd to Vine St
• Walk of Fame: Hollywood Blvd between Gower St & La Brea Ave, and Vine St between Yucca Ave & Sunset Blvd
• Hollywood & Highland: 6801 Hollywood Blvd
• Frederick's of Hollywood: 6751 Hollywood Blvd
• Capitol Records Tower: 1750 N Vine St

Top 10 Features

1. Walk of Fame
2. Musso and Frank Grill
3. Hollywood Roosevelt Hotel
4. TCL Chinese Theatre
5. El Capitan Theatre
6. Hollywood & Highland
7. The Egyptian Theatre
8. Pantages Theatre
9. Capitol Records Tower
10. Frederick's of Hollywood

1 Walk of Fame
Elvis, Lassie, and over 2,400 other celebs have been immortalized with a marble-encased brass star in the sidewalk *(above)*. Only those working in the movies, TV, radio, recording, or theater are eligible.

2 Musso and Frank Grill
During Hollywood's Golden Years, this restaurant was the haunt of stars such as Clark Gable and the Marks Brothers. Opened in 1919, it is the oldest restaurant in Hollywood and much of its classic interior remains unchanged *(see p101)*.

3 Hollywood Roosevelt Hotel
Douglas Fairbanks Sr. presided over the inaugural Academy Awards here *(below & p146)* in 1929 and Marilyn Monroe shot her first commercial by the pool, later adorned with blue squiggles by the artist David Hockney.

For more on Hollywood **See pp58–9**

4 TCL Chinese Theatre
The world's most famous movie theater *(below & p56)* opened in 1927 with a screening of Cecil B. De Mille's *King of Kings*. About 200 stars have left their hand- and foot-prints here, not to mention Betty Grable's famous legs.

7 The Egyptian Theatre
Now owned by the American Cinematheque, a nonprofit film organization, this 1922 theater is the birthplace of the "Hollywood premiere" *(see p56)*.

9 Capitol Records Tower
The world's first circular office building resembles a stack of records topped by a stylus that blinks out "Hollywood" in Morse code. It opened in 1956 as the head-quarters of the music giant, Capitol Records.

10 Frederick's of Hollywood
Started by entrepreneur Frederick Mellinger in 1946, this famous lingerie store has dressed Hollywood greats such as Garbo, West, and Monroe, and been responsible for innovations such as the push-up bra and thong.

5 El Capitan Theatre
The strikingly ornate El Capitan *(above & p56)* was Hollywood's first live theater and began screening films in 1941. Today, it functions as a Disney first-run movie theater.

6 Hollywood & Highland
This cornerstone of Hollywood revitalization combines shops, restaurants, night clubs, movie theaters, a hotel, and the 3,400-seat Dolby Theatre *(see p55)*, home of the Oscars.

8 Pantages Theatre
The grande dame of Tinseltown theaters sparkles once again in restored Art Deco glory. The lobby leads to the magnificent auditorium with its three-dimensional ceiling. It now hosts blockbuster Broadway shows *(see p55)*.

A Star for the Stars

A star on the Walk of Fame requires the prior approval of a screening committee appointed by the Hollywood Chamber of Commerce. Of the 200 applications received every year, only 10 percent get the nod – and the privilege to pay the $20,000 for installation and maintenance. Studios, and sometimes, fan clubs, usually foot the bill. Induction ceremonies are held once or twice a month and are open to the public. Check out www.hollywoodchamber.net for who's up next.

Guideline Tours (323-930-0749 or 1-800-60-GUIDE) offers tours in and around Hollywood

⁝10 The Getty Center

An exquisite art collection, superb architecture, and lovely gardens combine with a hilltop location to create one of LA's finest cultural destinations. Designed by Richard Meier, the Getty Center opened in December 1997 after 14 years of planning and construction. It unites the entities of the Getty Trust created by oil tycoon J. Paul Getty (1892–1976), including research and conservation institutes. At its core, however, is the museum with exquisite European art from illuminated manuscripts to Impressionist paintings, contemporary sculpture, and photography.

Steps leading to the Getty Museum

🍴 Bring your own picnic to enjoy along with the views in the gardens or courtyard, or pick up a light meal at a kiosk or the self-service café. For great gourmet meals, book a table at The Restaurant.

⭐ Unlike most art museums, the Getty welcomes kids with special children-oriented audio guides and a staffed Family Room filled with games and various hands-on activities.

Take advantage of the free architecture and garden tours that the Getty offers through the day.

• Map C2
• 1200 Getty Center Dr, Brentwood
• 310-440-7300
• Open 10am–5:30pm Tue–Sun (to 9pm Sat)
• Free, parking $15 ($10 after 5pm)
• www.getty.edu

Top 10 Artworks

1 Irises
2 Young Italian Woman at a Table
3 Wheatstacks, Snow Effect, Morning
4 The Calydonian Boar Hunt
5 The Abduction of Europa
6 Venus & Adonis
7 Christ's Entry into Brussels in 1889
8 La Promenade
9 Cabinet on Stand
10 The Adoration of the Magi

Irises
Van Gogh (1853–90) painted this exquisite work *(right)* in the last year of his life in a mental asylum. The intense color and energetic composition borrow from Gauguin and Japanese printmaker Hokusai.

Young Italian Woman at a Table
Cézanne's (1839–1906) emotionally charged painting of a melancholy young woman shows off his great versatility and technical prowess.

Wheatstacks, Snow Effect, Morning
This is one of 30 works which Claude Monet (1840–1926) painted between 1890 and 1891. Set against a soft sky and faintly visible houses, the wheatstacks are a solid, imposing presence *(right)*.

The Calydonian Boar Hunt
Rubens's (1577–1640) dynamic interpretation of the slaying of the Calydonian boar was painted in 1611. The work established the theme of the epic combat between man and animal, a subject to which the artist would later return.

The Getty Center's event calendar can be accessed at www.getty.edu/visit/calendar

6 Modern Rome, Campo Vaccino

Turner's atmospheric view of Rome from the Capitoline Hill *(left)* is the last of his Roman paintings. It ably shows why this English artist (1775–1851) was celebrated as the "painter of light".

9 Cabinet on Stand

This cabinet *(above)* celebrates the triumphs of the French king, Louis XIV. Attributed to André-Charles Boulle (1642–1732), pewter and tortoiseshell are some of the materials used.

10 The Adoration of the Magi

In this Renaissance masterpiece, Andrea Mantegna (c.1431–1506) emulates the compact composition of ancient Roman reliefs to achieve a sense of intimacy between subjects. The three kings represent Europe, Asia, and Africa.

5 The Abduction of Europa

Rembrandt (1606–69) found great inspiration in Ovid's *Metamorphoses*. This work *(below)* captures a dramatic moment: Jupiter, disguised as a white bull, spirits away the princess Europa across the oceans.

7 Christ's Entry into Brussels in 1889

Belgian James Ensor's (1860–1949) painting is one of the most controversial works of the 19th century. The grotesque scene reflects the artist's uneasiness with contemporary society.

8 La Promenade

An homage to his favorite artists such as Watteau and Courbet, this early Impressionist painting by Renoir (1841–1919) shows a young couple coyly heading for the woods.

Getty Villa

In a separate location on the Pacific Coast Highway, this museum and educational center houses over 1,200 Greek, Roman, and Etruscan antiquities dating from 6,500 BC to AD 400. On display are sculptures, everyday artifacts, and treasures such as Cycladic figures. Six galleries on the second floor are devoted to changing exhibitions.
• *17985 Pacific Coast Highway*
• *310-440-7300*
• *Open 10am–5pm Wed–Mon*
• *Advance timed ticket required, parking $15*

The Getty's self-guided audio tour is offered in several languages, including Spanish, English, and Chinese. Children's tours also available

13

Left **Electric Tram** Center **Panoramic Views** Right **Central Garden**

Top 10 Features of the Getty

1 Electric Tram
The Getty experience kicks off with a smooth five-minute ride up the hill from the entrance gate to the Arrival Plaza in a driver-less, computer-operated tram.

2 Panoramic Views
On clear days, the views from the Getty's hilltop perch are spectacular, especially around sunset. Take in the vastness of LA's labyrinthine streets, the Santa Monica Mountains, and the Pacific Ocean.

3 Central Garden
These beautiful, constantly changing gardens were designed by visual artist Robert Irwin (b.1928). Wander along tree-lined paths and across a gentle stream to a reflecting pool with floating azaleas and ringed by beautiful specialty gardens.

4 Shopping and Dining
There are plenty of options for a day-long visit, including the Museum Store and shops devoted to Impressionism, photography, and the latest exhibits. For refreshments, try the restaurant, café, kiosks, or gourmet picnics.

5 Decorative Arts
The Getty's famous collection of French decorative art and furniture from the 17th and 18th centuries is displayed in a series of period rooms. The paneled Régence salon from 1710 is a must-see.

6 Illuminated Manuscripts
Shown on a rotating basis, the Getty's collection of illuminated manuscripts covers the entire Middle Ages and Renaissance. The *Stammheim Missal* (1120) from Germany is among the most prized.

7 Drawings
Highlights of this collection, dating from the 14th to the 19th centuries, include Albrecht Dürer's exquisite *The Stag Beetle* (1505) and Leonardo da Vinci's *Studies for the Christ Child with Lamb* (c.1503–06).

8 Photography
Known for its images from the early 1840s, this department's collection concentrates on work by European and American artists. Man Ray's *Tears* is among the most famous pieces.

9 European Painting
The museum's collection of European paintings is small but choice. Paintings from the Italian Renaissance and Baroque periods, as well as French Impressionism, are particularly well represented.

10 Outdoor Sculpture
Works by many of the 20th century's greatest sculptors are displayed throughout the grounds. The sculptures, including work by Henry Moore, Alberto Giacometti, Roy Lichtenstein, and Joan Miró, were donated by the late film producer Ray Stark and his wife, Fran.

Top 10 Building Statistics

1. Campus size: 24 acres
2. Campus altitude: 900 ft (275 m)
3. Cost: $1 billion
4. Cubic yards (of earth) moved: 1.5 million
5. Travertine used: 16,000 tons
6. Weight of each travertine block: 250 pounds (126 kg)
7. Enameled aluminum panels: 40,000
8. Exterior glass: 164,650 sq ft (14,820 sq m)
9. Number of doors: 3,200
10. Length of tram ride: 0.75 miles (1.2 km)

The Architecture

Roosting on its hilltop site on the edge of the Santa Monica Mountains, the Getty Center is an imposing presence, far removed from city noise and bustle. An amazing feat of architecture and engineering,

Detail of façade

it was designed by New York-based Modernist Richard Meier (b.1934), an internationally acclaimed architect who also drafted the Paley Center for Media in Beverly Hills (see p111). For the Getty, Meier arranged the main buildings along two natural ridges connected by creative landscaping. Curvilinear elements, such as in the Museum Entrance Hall, combine with angular structures to create an effect of fluidity and openness. This is further enhanced by the use of travertine, a honey-colored stone quarried in Italy, which covers most buildings. Many of the stones bear fossilized leaves and feathers.

A Modern "Acropolis"

Seen from above, the Getty Center looks like a bunker atop a hill. But once you're within, walking beneath curvilinear balconies, across acres of rich gleaming stone, and through wondrous green gardens, you begin to see the Getty as a sort of modern – and thoroughly American – "Acropolis": classic and timeless.

The Getty's distinctive curvilinear architecture

Los Angeles County Museum of Art (LACMA)

The largest encyclopedic art museum in the western US, LACMA was founded in 1910 and moved to its present Miracle Mile home in 1965. Its treasure trove includes paintings by Dürer, Monet, and Picasso; American and Latin American art; and works from the Middle East and Asia. A lively schedule of concerts, lectures, and film screenings makes LACMA a community destination. The Broad Contemporary Art Museum (BCAM) opened in 2008; public spaces, gardens, and a building to house special exhibitions have subsequently been added.

Ceci n'est pas une pipe by René Magritte, 1928

Good places to rest are the Plaza Café, which serves light meals and refreshments, and Ray's Restaurant, with farm-to-table dining and an outdoor bar.

Free jazz concerts draw a sizable crowd on Friday nights (5:30–8:30pm) from April to December. The free Sunday chamber music series is also quite popular.

- Map N6
- 5905 Wilshire Blvd, Midtown
- 323-857-6000
- Open 11am–5pm Mon, Tue, & Thu, 11am–8pm Fri, 10am–7pm Sat & Sun
- Adm adults $15, seniors & students $10, free for under 17s, free second Tue of the month, extra charge for special exhibits
- www.lacma.org

Top 10 Collections

1. American Art
2. Ancient & Islamic Art
3. Modern & Contemporary Art
4. Chinese & Korean Art
5. Japanese Art
6. South & Southeast Asian Art
7. Latin American Art
8. European Painting & Sculpture
9. Photography and Prints & Drawings
10. Decorative Arts & Design

Ahmanson Building

Resnick Pavillion

LACMA West

American Art

This collection offers a survey of American art from the 1700s to the 1940s. Among the highlights are works by late 19th-century figurative artists such as Winslow Homer. Other works include paintings by George Bellows and Mary Cassatt, specifically *Mother About to Wash her Sleepy Child* (above).

Ancient & Islamic Art

LACMA's Art of the Ancient World collection spans more than 4,000 years and features horse trappings, stone reliefs, and pottery. The museum's renowned Islamic Art section covers a wide range of art forms.

Every Tuesday at 1pm, the museum presents a classic film in the Bing Theater

3 Modern & Contemporary Art

Matisse, Picasso, and Magritte are among the artists represented in the Modern Art section. LACMA's collection of contemporary art spans from 1945 to the present and ranges from paintings to video installations.

4 Chinese & Korean Art

The largest permanent space devoted to Korean art outside of South Korea displays work from the 5th to the 20th century. Chinese works include ceramics, paintings, and ancient bronzes.

5 Japanese Art

The Pavilion for Japanese Art is the only building outside Japan solely devoted to its art. It houses superb Edo-period paintings and exquisite porcelain.

8 European Painting & Sculpture

An exquisite collection that encompasses works by Flemish and Dutch masters and French Impressionists, including Monet's *In the Woods at Giverny (above).*

9 Photography and Prints & Drawings

The photography collection focuses mainly on images produced in the last 60 years, while the Prints & Drawings exhibition displays artworks from the 15th century to the present day.

10 Decorative Arts & Design

This area has European and American furniture, metalwork, and glass from the Middle Ages to today. The Palevsky Arts and Crafts collection is very comprehensive.

Pavilion for Japanese Art

Hammer Building

Bing Center

Art of the Americas Building

Entrance Pavilion

Broad Contemporary Art Museum Building

Key

■	Lower Level
■	Plaza Level
■	Second Level
■	Third Level

6 South & Southeast Asian Art

This collection is one of the finest, with stone sculpture, watercolors, drawings, illustrated manuscripts, ritual art, and coins from the 11th to the 20th century. Among the highlights are Indian art and sculpture *(above).*

7 Latin American Art

These galleries feature ancient American, Spanish colonial, modern, and contemporary works. Key acquisitions range from Mayan works to those of Alys, Orozco, Wifredo Lam, and Torres-Garcia.

Gallery Guide

LACMA's permanent collection is displayed in five buildings. European painting and sculpture, ancient and Islamic art, and south and southeast Asian art are in the Ahmanson Building. The Hammer Building houses Chinese and Korean art, photography, prints, and drawings. Next door is the Pavilion for Japanese Art and, across the courtyard, is the Art of the Americas building with American and Latin American art and decorative arts and design. The Broad houses modern and contemporary art.

LACMA's Art Rental & Sales Gallery is located on the lower level of the Bing Center

Left **LACMA** Center *Untitled Improvisation III* Right *The Magdalen with the Smoking Flame*

Top 10 LACMA Masterpieces

1 Portrait of Mrs Edward L. Davis & Her Son, Livingston Davis

John Singer Sargent (1856–1925) was a gifted and prolific East Coast society portrait painter. This 1890 work blends loose brushwork (the boy) with stark realism (the woman's head).

2 Standing Warrior

Standing about 3-ft (1-m) tall, this figure of a king or warrior is the largest known effigy from western Mexico and was fired in one piece. It dates from between 200 BC and AD 300.

"Standing Warrior"

3 Eagle-headed Deity

Ancient Syrian palaces were often decorated with intricately carved stone slabs. This one depicts a deity in the process of fertilizing a tree by scattering pollen from a pail.

4 Shiva as the Lord of Dance

This exquisite sculpture from the 11th century portrays the Hindu god Shiva as the source of cosmic dance, which defines the universe as a cycle of creation, preservation, and destruction.

5 Untitled Improvisation III

A pioneer of pure abstract painting, Russian-born Wassily Kandinsky (1866–1944) imbued his canvasses with spirituality expressed through shapes and bold colors, as in this 1914 work.

6 Flower Day

Mexican artist Diego Rivera (1886–1957) is best known for his murals and as Frida Kahlo's husband, but the famous *Flower Day* (1925) shows off his talent as a Cubist-influenced painter.

7 The Magdalen with the Smoking Flame

French Baroque artist Georges de la Tour (1593–1652) employs deep contrasts between light and shadow to depict his subject with great intimacy and realism.

8 Yama and Yami

At nearly 2.4-m (8-ft) high, this is one of the largest Tibetan thangka paintings outside Tibet. The painting dates from the late 17th to early 18th century and has undergone extensive restoration.

9 Mulholland Drive

LA-based British artist David Hockney created many panoramic paintings such as this brightly colored and dynamically composed one. This 1980 work shows the famous LA road linking the artist's house and studio.

10 Chest of Drawers

Gold and silver leaf embellish a surface composed of dozens of coats of lacquer on this masterful chest showing famous scenes around Lake Biwa. It was made by Yamamoto Shunsho in 18th-century Kyoto.

Discover more at www.dk.com

Top 10 of Art Deco on the Miracle Mile

1. May Co. Department Store (now LACMA West), 1940: Wilshire at Fairfax Ave
2. El Rey Theater (1928): 5517 Wilshire Blvd
3. Desmonds Department Store Building (1929): 5514 Wilshire Blvd
4. Commercial Building (1927): 5464 Wilshire Blvd
5. Roman's Food Mart (1935): 5413 Wilshire Blvd
6. Chandler's Shoe Store (1938): Wilshire at Cloverdale Ave
7. Dominguez-Wilshire Blvd (1930): 5410 Wilshire Blvd
8. The Dark Room (1938): 5370 Wilshire Blvd
9. Wilson Building (1930): 5217-5231 Wilshire Blvd
10. Security Pacific Bank Building (1929): 5209 Wilshire Blvd

Museum Row
With its four museums, including LACMA, the western end of Miracle Mile is also known as "Museum Row."

The Miracle Mile

LACMA sits on a particularly interesting and historic stretch of Wilshire Boulevard. The so-called "Miracle Mile" was LA's first shopping district outside of Downtown and the first ever designed with easy access for the motorized shopper. The man behind this vision was developer A.W. Ross who, in 1921, bought 18 acres of land between La Brea Boulevard and Fairfax Avenue with the lofty goal of turning it into a "Fifth Avenue of the West." His plan succeeded wildly, as department stores and upscale retail establishments quickly moved in, but it also marked the beginning of LA's decentralization. By the 1960s, however, a new innovation – the shopping mall – spelled the end of the "miracle." Although a shadow of its former self, the Miracle Mile has been revitalized to some extent with galleries attracting their share of the hip lot. A few of the Art Deco buildings have survived and are now on the National Register of Historic Places.

The Miracle Mile sign

May Company building (now LACMA West)

The Los Angeles Art Deco Society (310-659-3326) offers walking tours of the Miracle Mile

TOP 10 El Pueblo de Los Angeles

This historic district protects LA's oldest structures, all built between 1818 and 1926. Close to the site where 44 Mexican men, women, and children established El Pueblo de Los Angeles in the name of the Spanish crown in 1781, it also reflects the heritage of other ethnic groups that arrived later, including the Chinese, Italians, and French. As LA grew into a metropolis, businesses relocated to newer neighborhoods and the area plunged into deep decline. Now beautifully restored, three of its 27 structures contain museums.

Olvera Street marketplace

🚶 Olvera Street is a great place for an authentic Mexican meal. Try the popular Casa Golondrina or the more casual La Luz del Dia.

🕐 Volunteer docents offer free guided tours of El Pueblo at 10am, 11am, and noon Tuesday to Saturday. Check in next to the firehouse. The visitor center offers self-guided tour pamphlets.

• Map W4
• El Pueblo Visitor Center: Avila Adobe Museum, Olvera Street, 213-628-1274, Open 9am–4pm daily, www.elpueblo.lacity.org
• Olvera Street market: Open 10am–7pm daily (some shops may open earlier and close later)
• Avila Adobe: Open 9am–4pm daily, free
• Old Plaza Firehouse: Open 10am–3pm daily, free
• Chinese American Museum: 425 N Los Angeles St, Open 10am–3pm Tue–Sun, Adm $3

Top 10 Sights

1. Olvera Street
2. América Tropical
3. Sepulveda House
4. Avila Adobe
5. Blessing of the Animals
6. Plaza Catholic Church
7. Old Plaza
8. Old Plaza Firehouse
9. Pico House
10. Chinese American Museum

1 Olvera Street
Named after LA's first county judge, this bustling, brick-paved lane has been a Mexican marketplace since 1930. Wander past colorful carts overflowing with folk art and curios or try some tasty tacos and *tortas*.

2 América Tropical
El Pueblo is home to a rare mural by Mexican artist David Alfaro Siqueiros. Painted in 1932, this controversial work is a visceral allegory about the exploitation of Mexican workers.

3 Sepulveda House
Eloisa Sepulveda built this lovely Victorian house *(above)* in 1887 as her home, a hotel, and stores. Today, it contains El Pueblo's visitor center.

4 Avila Adobe
LA's oldest surviving house *(below)* was built by mayor Don Francisco Avila in 1818 and went through several incarnations as a military headquarters and boarding house. The restored rooms offer a glimpse of 1840s life.

The information booth at 130 Paseo de la Plaza offers free guided walking tours

7 Old Plaza

Music, dancing, and merriment fills the Old Plaza *(left)* during lively fiestas. Sculptures of King Carlos III of Spain and Felipe de Neve, and a plaque listing the names of El Pueblo's original settlers, honor LA's founders.

9 Pico House

Pío Pico, the last Mexican governor of California, built this grand Italianate edifice *(above)* in 1870. It was LA's first three-story structure and once housed a hotel.

10 Chinese American Museum

The Chinese first settled in and around El Pueblo in the late 19th century. This museum, housed in the 1890s Garnier Building, traces the community's history.

5 Blessing of the Animals

Leo Politi's endearing 1978 mural *(above)* shows the centuries-old Mexican tradition of thanking animals – canaries to cows – for the joy and service they provide humans. Celebrations take place in the Old Plaza each year.

6 Plaza Catholic Church

Worshipers have gathered in LA's oldest church since 1822. The original was rebuilt in 1861, with several subsequent alterations. Features include the painted ceiling and the main altar framed in gold leaf *(right)*.

8 Old Plaza Firehouse

This two-story brick building is a must-see. Firehouse No.1 with its all-volunteer crew and horse-drawn equipment remained operational until 1897. Check out a small exhibit of fire-fighting memorabilia.

The Mother of Olvera Street

Had it not been for Christine Sterling (1881–1963), an LA socialite turned civic activist, the El Pueblo de Los Angeles area would still remain a railway station. Dismayed by the seediness of LA's oldest neighborhood, Sterling launched her 1926 campaign to save it. Her dedication earned her the backing of *LA Times* publisher Harry Chandler and others. In April 1930, Olvera Street was reincarnated as a bustling Mexican market. The Avila Adobe contains an exhibit on Sterling's triumph.

Huntington Library, Art Collections, & Botanical Gardens

The Huntington is one of those rare places that manages to please the eye, stimulate the mind, and nourish the soul all at the same time. The former estate of railroad and real estate baron Henry E. Huntington (1850–1927), it consists of a trio of treasures: the art collections include fine examples of British, French, and American art; the Huntington Library has about seven million rare manuscripts and books, including a Gutenberg Bible; and the Botanical Gardens are a fantastic feast of flora in a pleasing parklike setting.

Huntington Library

○ Picnicking is not permitted, but a self-service restaurant offers light meals and refreshments. Better yet, make reservations (626-683-8131) for English tea served in the Rose Garden Room, a time-honored Huntington tradition.

✿ Amazing plants from the Huntington nursery are available for purchase during the Garden Talk and Sale event held every second Thursday of the month.

• Map F2
• 1151 Oxford Rd, San Marino near Pasadena
• 626-405-2100
• Open noon–4:30pm Mon, Wed–Fri, 10:30am–4:30pm Sat–Sun, 10:30am–4:30pm Wed–Sun in summer
• Adm adults $20 ($23 at w/ends); seniors $15 ($18 at w/ends); students 12–18 $12 ($13 at w/ends); children 5–11 $8; under 5s free

Top 10 Features

1. Japanese Garden
2. Desert Garden
3. Chaucer's "The Canterbury Tales"
4. Gutenberg Bible
5. Rose Garden
6. Chinese Garden
7. North Vista
8. Greene & Greene Exhibit
9. Boone Gallery
10. Camellia Garden

Japanese Garden
A place for strolling and quiet contemplation, Huntington's Japanese Garden *(right)* is among America's oldest of its kind. Its canyon setting is accented by a shimmering pond filled with *koi* fish and water lilies, a waterfall, and a teahouse.

Desert Garden
This exotic garden *(below)*, with its clusters of whimsical cacti and flowering succulents, has an otherworldly feel. One of the world's finest, it's a study of the ways in which desert plants adapt to survive in harsh conditions.

Chaucer's "The Canterbury Tales"
This rare 1410 manuscript of English poet Geoffrey Chaucer's most famous work is complete, in marvelous condition, and filled with luminous illustrations. It's perhaps better known as the "Ellesmere Manuscript," after its former owner, the Earl of Ellesmere.

For useful information on the Huntington log on to www.huntington.org

Los Angeles Top 10

Gutenberg Bible

The Huntington Library's star exhibit, this 1455 Bible *(left)* is one of only 12 surviving copies printed on vellum (calf or sheep skin) by Johannes Gutenberg of Mainz, Germany, the inventor of movable type. The colorful chapter headings and decorations were added by hand.

Greene & Greene Exhibit

Charles and Henry Greene, known for their wooden houses and fine furnishings, were the first to practice the early 20th-century Craftsman style *(see p91)*.

Boone Gallery

The Boone Gallery began life in 1911 as Henry Huntington's garage. With columns that echo the Neo-Classical style of the mansion, it is used for housing temporary exhibitions.

Camellia Garden

Camellias reached the Western world in the 18th century. With about 1,200 varieties (in bloom from January to March), this garden has one of the finest collections.

A Short Guide

Access the Huntington from either Orlando Road or Oxford Road. Both lead to a large parking lot and from there to the entrance pavilion, where you can pick up a free map. An excellent museum store stocks art books and quality gifts. While you can "do" the Huntington in an hour or two, it's really the kind of place that is meant to be savored. Come early and spend the day.

Chinese Garden

This garden, Liu Fang Yuan, the Garden of Flowering Fragrance, was inspired by the Chinese tradition of using gardens for scholarly purposes. Liu Fang Yuan features a complex of pavilions, bridges, and a teahouse, encircling a small lake.

Rose Garden

This romantic garden *(above)* brings you nearly 1,200 rose varieties, some of them with a pedigree going back to ancient Greece. These noble blossoms may be enjoyed from March right through December. May is the peak month.

North Vista

The palms and stone statues lining the central lawn of this Baroque garden remind one of European palaces. It connects the Huntington Gallery with a dolphin-studded Italian fountain against a San Gabriel mountain backdrop.

Left **Huntington Art Gallery** Center *Chimborazo* Right *The Long Leg*

Top 10 Huntington Artworks

1 Blue Boy
Thomas Gainsborough (1727–88) was the most sought-after portrait painter of British high society. This famous 1770 painting shows Jonathan Buttall, a friend of the artist, in 17th-century costume.

2 Pinkie
Thomas Lawrence (1769–1830) painted Sarah Barrett Moulton, nicknamed "Pinkie," aged 11, in a refreshingly direct and lively manner. She died shortly after the completion of this painting, possibly of consumption.

3 View on the Stour near Dedham
Romantic landscape painter John Constable (1776–1837) adopted a lyrical approach to depicting nature. His emphasis on sky, light, and other intangible qualities greatly influenced other artists, including the Impressionists.

4 Madonna and Child
A master of early Flemish painting, Rogier van der Weyden (1400–64) infused his works with emotional intensity, evident here in the Virgin's face and hands.

5 The Grand Canal, Venice
This 1837 painting is a fine example of the translucency typical of the works of J.M.W. Turner (1775–1851). The tiny person in the lower right corner is Shylock from the play *The Merchant of Venice*.

6 The Western Brothers
John Singleton Copley (1738–1815) was born in Colonial Boston and moved to England just before 1776. This 1783 double portrait is characterized by flowing strokes and strong expressions on the faces of the young men.

7 Chimborazo
A trip to Ecuador inspired this painting by 19th-century American landscape artist, Frederic Church (1826–1900). Church took creative license when compressing the mountains, desert, and jungle into a single image.

8 Breakfast in Bed
Pennsylvania-born Mary Cassatt (1844–1926) moved to Paris in 1873, where she befriended Edgar Degas and fell under the spell of Impressionism. The subject of mother and child was a favorite.

Madonna and Child by Rogier van der Weyden (1400–64)

The Huntington's Virginia Steele Scott Gallery displays American art from the colonial period through to the mid-20th century

9 The Long Leg

The solitude and anonymity of human existence is a recurring theme in the paintings of Edward Hopper (1882–1967), a leading 20th-century American Realist. Here, these sentiments of loneliness are expressed in a famous sailing scene.

10 The Robinson Dining Room

This recreated dining room exemplifies the innovative genius of the brothers Charles and Henry Greene. Designed between 1905 and 1907, it contains original furniture and an amazing chandelier.

Huntington Art Gallery First Floor Plan

Huntington Art Gallery Second Floor Plan

The Scott Galleries of American Art First Floor Plan

Top 10 Big Red Cars Facts & Stats

1 Covered four counties
2 Linked 50 communities
3 First ride: 1901
4 Last ride: 1961
5 Track: 1,150 miles (1,850 km)
6 Fleet: 900 cars at peak
7 Passengers: 109 million in 1944 (peak year)
8 Fare: a penny a mile
9 Top speed: 40–50 mph (60–80 km/h)
10 Car length: 50 ft (15 m)

Henry Huntington's Big Red Cars

Henry E. Huntington made his vast fortune by marrying real estate speculation with public transportation. The largest landowner in Southern California, he established the Pacific Electric Railway in 1901, primarily to get people out to the far-flung new suburbs he was developing. Soon Huntington's fleet of interurban red trolleys – dubbed the "Big Red Cars" – became the world's largest electric-transit system, linking communities throughout Southern California. By the time he sold most of his holdings to the Southern Pacific Railroad in 1910, the population of LA had tripled to around 310,000. "The last trolley" made its farewell voyage in 1961.

Pacific Electric Engine on display in Travel Town, Griffith Park

The Lois and Robert F. Erburu Gallery was added to the Virginia Steele Scott Gallery of American Art in 2005

Universal Studios Hollywood℠

The world's largest movie and television studio sprang from the imagination of cinema pioneer Carl Laemmle. In 1915 he bought a former chicken ranch, brought in cameras, lights, and actors, and started making silent films. The theme park began taking shape in 1964. Today, Universal Studios Hollywood℠ gets more visitors (about five million a year) than any other attraction in LA County. Among the studio's greatest film hits are Jurassic Park (1993) and Shrek (2001).

Shrek 4-D™
The award-winning hit *Shrek* comes to life in this state-of-the-art attraction featuring ground-breaking *OgreVision* animation and sensory immersion. Voice-overs include comic talents Eddie Murphy, Mike Myers, and Cameron Diaz.

The Universal Studios Hollywood℠ sign

- Dining inside the park is limited to snack bars and self-service restaurants. For a sit-down meal, get your hand stamped for re-entry and head to CityWalk's many superb restaurants.

- Beat the crowds with the Front-of-the-Line Ticket or the guided VIP Experience, which includes an expanded Studio Tour (tours also run daily in Spanish). Prices vary.

- Map D2
- 100 Universal City Plaza, Universal City
- 800-UNIVERSAL
- Seasonal hours vary. Call for details.
- Adm adults $84; adults or children under 4 ft (1.2 m) tall $76; under 3s free; discounted tickets available online
- Print-at-home ticketing is available at www.universalstudios hollywood.com

Top 10 Features
1. Studio Tour
2. Revenge of The Mummy℠ – The Ride
3. The Simpsons Ride™
4. Shrek 4-D™
5. King Kong
6. Jurassic Park® – The Ride
7. Transformers™: The Ride 3-D
8. Water World®
9. CityWalk
10. Meeting the "Stars"

Studio Tour
For a look at movie-making, this 45-minute narrated tram tour of the actual working studio is a must. Cruise past 35 soundstages to the vast backlot with its fabled outdoor sets *(right)*.

Revenge of The Mummy℠ – The Ride
The park's first ever roller coaster is a psychological thrill ride that will bring you face to face with the fear of darkness, of insects, of speed, and of heights.

The Simpsons Ride™
Join the Simpsons in a cartoon theme park called Krustyland as they try to save Bart from Sideshow Bob. This ride features 29 characters from the popular TV show, all voiced by the original actors.

King Kong
The King Kong 360 3-D is the first theme park attraction created by Peter Jackson, who directed the Oscar-winning 2005 film upon which it is based. Guests on the Universal tram are given 3-D glasses and enter into a world where the film and tram are tied into a motion simulator that creates a titanic struggle between the 9.1 m- (30 ft-) tall gorilla and gigantic dinosaurs. It's billed as "the largest, most intense 3-D experience on the planet."

Note: *The simulated earthquakes and floods in the tram tour may be rather frightening for very young children*

Lower Lot
Escalator Down to Lower Lot
2
3
6
5
1
Upper Lot
Blast Zone
4
The Blues Brothers
7
Universal Amphitheatre
8
Entrance
9
Universal Citywalk

Jurassic Park® – The Ride
A gentle rafting trip through a lush primordial park inhabited by cloned dinosaurs turns into a nightmare as guests come face to face with a voracious T-Rex *(above)*. The only escape is an 84-ft (25-m) plunge that leaves everyone drenched.

CityWalk
A lively carnival atmosphere reigns along this studio-adjacent promenade with its mix of restaurants, shops, and entertainment venues. The best time to visit is after sunset when huge neon signs turn CityWalk into a miniature Las Vegas Strip.

Meeting the "Stars"
Chances of running into a real celebrity are slim, but don't fret – there'll be plenty of photo ops with actors dressed as classic silver screen stars such as Charlie Chaplin or even some favorite cartoon characters.

Studio Guide

Universal Studios is divided into upper and lower sections linked by a multi-segmented escalator, the world's second longest. All visitors receive an orientation map that also lists that day's show times. Note that it's about a 10-minute stroll along CityWalk from the parking lot to the box office. The park is least busy midweek in the off-season (October to April). In summer, arrive before doors open and race to the most popular attractions first.

Water World®
For the best stunts, catch this show *(below)* where the polar ice caps have melted and all land lies beneath the sea. Memorable moments include a crash-landing seaplane and fireballs.

Transformers™: The Ride 3-D
Get caught in an inter-galactic war between the heroic Autobots *(above)* and the evil Decepticons in this popular ride that uses sophisticated special effects and elaborate flight simulation technology.

10 Griffith Park

Griffith Park is a 4,000-acre natural playground of rugged hills and gentle valleys, draped with native oak trees, manzanita, and sage and crisscrossed by hiking and horseback trails. The country's largest urban park owes its existence to the Welsh Griffith Jenkins Griffith (1850–1919). In 1896, Griffith donated a large portion of his estate to the city with the proviso that it become "a place of recreation and rest for the masses." Today, the park is filled with picnic areas, golf courses, and tennis courts.

Old steam locomotive, Travel Town Museum

🍴 The leafy oasis of Fern Dell is good for picnics, while the Crossroads West Café at the Autry National Center serves breakfast and lunch.

🐎 Sunset Ranch Stables (3400 Beachwood Drive) leads Friday night horseback rides through Griffith Park.

- Map D1
- Griffith Park: Open 6am–10pm
- Griffith Park Ranger Station: 4730 Crystal Springs Dr • Griffith Observatory: 2800 E Observatory Rd, 213-473-0800, Open noon–10pm Tue–Fri, 10am–10pm Sat–Sun
- Autry National Center: 4700 Western Heritage Way, Open 10am–5pm Tue–Sun (to 8pm Thu)
- Travel Town Museum: 5200 Zoo Dr, Open 10am–4pm daily (to 5pm Sat–Sun) • Bronson Caves: Take Canyon Dr to the end, then take the path past the gate east of the last parking lot
- Southern Railroad: Open 10am–4:30pm Mon–Fri (to 5pm Sat–Sun)

Top 10 Features

1. Griffith Observatory & Planetarium
2. Greek Theatre
3. Mt. Hollywood Trail
4. Merry-Go-Round
5. Los Angeles Zoo
6. Autry National Center
7. Travel Town Museum
8. Forest Lawn Memorial Park – Hollywood Hills
9. Bronson Caves
10. Griffith Park & Southern Railroad

1 Griffith Observatory & Planetarium

The observatory *(right)* has been the park's chief attraction since 1935. A $93-million renovation project has added 40,000 sq ft (3716 sq m) of public space and a 300-seat state-of-the-art planetarium theater.

2 Greek Theatre

A favorite LA outdoor concert venue, the 1930 Greek Theatre *(above & p54)* presents a summer season of top musical talent in its leafy natural bowl setting. With almost 5,700 seats, it's great for close-ups of legends.

3 Mount Hollywood Trail

The popular trek to the top of Mount Hollywood, the highest point in Griffith Park, rewards hikers with plenty of exercise and sweeping views of Los Angeles *(below)*. Trailheads are located at Fern Dell and the Observatory.

For more information on Griffith Park log on to www.laparks.org/dos/parks/griffithpk

Merry-Go-Round
A slice of nostalgia in the midst of futuristic LA, this beloved 1926 Stillman carousel *(above)* has 68 exquisitely carved horses complete with real horse-hair tails.

Travel Town Museum
A good-sized fleet of vintage locomotives, freight and passenger cars, and several cabooses (goods trains) draw railroad aficionados to this outdoor museum. Children love riding the miniature train.

Griffith Park & Southern Railroad
Generations of children have boarded the three miniature trains that chug along a 1-mile (1.6-km) track *(above)* past pony rides, a Wild West ghost town, a Native American village, moving over a bridge, and through a tunnel, past grazing goats and a cactus garden.

Los Angeles Zoo
Some 1,200 animals are found here *(above & p51)*, including koalas and chimps. The breeding program has brought the California condor back from near-extinction.

Autry National Center
This great collection of art, artifacts, and memorabilia demystifies the history and mythology of the American West. Star exhibits include a Colt handgun collection.

Forest Lawn Memorial Park – Hollywood Hills
Buster Keaton and Bette Davis are among the celebrities interred in this parklike cemetery dotted with patriotic art and architecture. It was founded in 1917 by Hubert Eaton, who invented the "full-service cemetery" concept satirized by Evelyn Waugh.

Bronson Caves
Scenes from *Star Trek*, *Batman*, *Bonanza*, and countless other film and TV productions were shot in this former rock quarry and its caves. Tucked away in a remote corner of Griffith Park, it requires a short hike.

James Dean Memorial
James Dean was one of Hollywood's most dashing movie stars when, at age 24, he died in a car crash on a lone highway in Central California. A bronze bust outside the Griffith Park Observatory commemorates the actor, who filmed the famous knife-fight from *Rebel Without a Cause* on the steps of the building. The scene's intensity stems partly from the fact that the actors used real switchblades, though wearing protective vests. Look for Dean's bust on the west side of the lawn in front of the observatory.

ᴺᴼ10 Disneyland® Resort

From 1955 onwards, the landmarks of Disneyland® – the Matterhorn, Sleeping Beauty's Castle, and New Orleans Square – have been as familiar and as "real" as the Eiffel Tower or the Empire State Building. A second theme park, Disney's California Adventure™, has been added adjacent to the original. Downtown Disney®, a further addition, is an outdoor entertainment, restaurant, and retail district. Together with the two parks and three Disney hotels, Downtown Disney® forms the enormous complex called Disneyland® Resort.

Sleeping Beauty's Castle

🌐 Try the alfresco Italian at Wine Country Trattoria in Disney's California Adventure™, and Cajun fare at the candle-lit Blue Bayou in Disneyland®.

🎡 If you're staying in LA and want to be first through the gate when the parks open at 8am or 9am, leave at least 90 minutes early to avoid traffic.

• Map G5
• 1313 Harbor Blvd, Anaheim, about 30 miles (48 km) south of LA
• 714-781-4565
• Seasonal hours
• www.disneyland.com
• Disneyland®: 8am–10pm Mon–Fri, 8am–11pm or midnight Sat–Sun, Adm $69/$59 for adult/child 3–9
• California Adventure: 10am–6pm Mon–Fri, 10am–9pm Sat–Sun, Adm $87/$81 for adult/child 3–9
• Off-peak Disneyland®: 9am–6pm Mon–Fri, 9am–8pm Sat–Sun

Top 10 Attractions

1. Pirates of the Caribbean
2. Haunted Mansion
3. Indiana Jones Adventure™
4. Matterhorn Bobsleds
5. Splash Mountain
6. Big Thunder Mountain Railroad
7. Star Tours
8. Meeting Mickey
9. Roger Rabbit's Car Toon Spin
10. The Little Mermaid

1 Pirates of the Caribbean
Hold on to your hat as you plunge down into a watery world of darkness where wicked pirates plunder a Caribbean village *(right)*. Characters from the film include captains Jack Sparrow and Barbossa.

2 Haunted Mansion
Dare to enter the netherworld of this mysterious mansion in New Orleans Square inhabited by 999 ghoulish spirits. Board a "Doom Buggy" for a chilling ride and beware of hitchhiking ghosts. A perennial favorite.

3 Indiana Jones Adventure™
Join Indy in his battle against the forces of evil on this bumpy adventure ride through an old temple in Adventureland. Clamped into a rickety jeep, you'll plunge into deep caverns, skirt fiery lava, and escape from being crushed by a scary giant boulder.

4 Matterhorn Bobsleds
The park's first roller coaster *(left)* may look tame but it packs a surprising punch. Strap yourself into a double-seater bobsled for a bumpy but exhilarating race down and through the mountain. A must-do for kids! In Fantasyland.

Note: *Prices of Disneyland® tickets increase annually; discounted multi-day and multi-park passes are available*

Splash Mountain
Follow Brer Rabbit and a cast of other characters from Disney's *Song of the South* on their adventures as you travel along an enchanting watery path aboard hollowed-out flume logs. The climactic final drop will leave you gasping, exultant...and wet. In Critter Country.

Big Thunder Mountain Railroad
Hop on to this runaway mine train roller coaster in Frontierland for a journey through the Wild West *(below)*. Charge through bat caverns, brave falling rocks, and encounter coyotes and other scaries.

Star Tours – The Adventures Continue
Inspired by the original Disneyland Star Tours®, this popular attraction features varied characters and destinations in 3D. With multiple odysseys, guests are unlikely to repeat the same adventure. In Tomorrowland.

Meeting Mickey
An audience with Mickey brings smiles to kids' faces. Before meeting Mr. Mouse up close and personal, you're invited to stroll through his house and garden and visit the set of one of his cartoons. In Mickey's Toontown.

Roger Rabbit's Car Toon Spin
Get ready for a ride on the wild side as you pilot a runaway cab through the wacky and fun world of Roger Rabbit. In Mickey's Toontown.

The Little Mermaid
Hop on board a giant clam and enter Ariel's undersea world. This ride features many of the film's scenes brought to life through animatronics.

Shows, Parades, & Pyrotechnics

The thrill rides may be the main draw, but there are actually plenty of other things to do, especially in summer and on weekends. Daily schedules vary but you may get to see Mickey's sensational parade on Main Street with its explosive music and decorated floats. The skies are ablaze for "Remember...", a fireworks extravaganza backed by popular songs from famous Disney movies. Another seasonal highlight is Fantasmic!, a 25-minute night time live action special effects show starring Mickey Mouse and a host of other favorite Disney characters. Special shows are also set for the Christmas holidays, Lunar New Year, and Halloween.

The map you'll get with your Disneyland® ticket will provide the specifics about the show schedule for the day

Left **Disneyland® street** Right **Toy Story Midway Mania**

Disneyland® Best of the Rest

1 Toy Story Midway Mania
Put on your 3D glasses and be transported to a world of classic American carnival-style games. Shoot darts at balloons, rings at aliens, eggs at barnyard targets, and more. Keep your wits about you and watch out for the special effects!

2 Soarin' over California
Lift off as you "fly" above the Golden Gate Bridge, Napa Valley vineyards, the Sierras, and other California landmarks in this virtual hang-gliding adventure. The most memorable ride at Disney's California Adventure™.

3 It's Tough to Be a Bug
Starring a cast of termites, stinkbugs, tarantulas, and other creepy crawlies, this 3D animated movie brims with special effects, some of them rather tactile and intense. Great fun, though not for the squeamish or small children. At Disney's California Adventure™.

4 California Screamin'
This scary spine-tingling roller coaster at Disney's California Adventure™ shoots you out like a cannon, then smoothly zooms you around the track, making a complete loop under the Paradise Pier sign. The "carnival meets rock'n'roll" soundtrack is a draw.

5 Grizzly River Run
Billed as the "world's highest, longest, and fastest," this thrilling whitewater raft ride takes you on a churning trip

Grizzly River Run

For reservations at Disney restaurants, call Disney Dining on 714-781-DINE

The lobby of the Grand Californian Hotel

through the Sierra Nevada foothills beneath a Grizzly bear-shaped mountaintop. You will get wet on this one! At Disney's California Adventure™.

Downtown Disney®
This admission-free outdoor promenade is perfect for wrapping up the day with some shopping, a nice meal, and live music at the popular House of Blues or the Jazz Kitchen. The huge World of Disney store has all your favorite souvenirs.

ESPN Zone
The ultimate destination for sports junkies, this Downtown Disney® fixture offers 35,000 sq ft (3,250 sq m) of nonstop action. More than 175 TV monitors sprinkled throughout broadcast different sporting events. The Sports Arena brims with sports-themed interactive, video, and virtual reality games.

Catal Restaurant & Uva Bar
For a culinary journey around the Mediterranean book a table at this Downtown Disney® outpost of star chef Joachim Splichal.

Downstairs at the Uva Bar it's mostly casual tapas, while upstairs the focus is on fine dining. Leave room for the *crème brulée*. § *1580 Disneyland Dr, Suite 103 (in Downtown Disney®) • 714-774-4442 • Veg: On request • $$*

Disney's Grand Californian
The nicest of the resort's three Disney hotels, the Grand Californian *(see p149)* carefully recreates the early 20th-century Craftsman style. The Great Hall lobby is canopied by a timbered ceiling and anchored by a large stone fireplace. A special bonus for kids and thrill seekers: a direct entry gate to Disney's California Adventure™.

Napa Rose Restaurant
Stained glass, murals, and a cosy fireplace contribute to the refined ambience at this award-winning restaurant where dinners every evening become exciting culinary celebrations. The menu, which changes seasonally, is complemented by an exceptional wine list. At Disney's Grand Californian Hotel *(see p149)*. § *1600 S Disneyland Dr • 714-635-2300 • Dinner only • $$$*

The Disneyland® Resort

🔟 Top 10 Practical Tips

1 When to Visit
The parks are busiest in summer, and around Easter, Thanksgiving, and between Christmas and New Year. Crowds thin out from January to March and November to mid-December.

2 Beating the Crowds
If visiting during peak periods, come midweek instead of weekends and arrive at least half an hour before gates open, then head for your favorite rides first. Lines are shorter during lunchtime and the parades.

3 FastPASS System
This excellent scheme significantly cuts down on wait times in both parks. Insert your admission ticket into machines outside select attractions to receive a voucher with a pre-assigned one-hour time slot for faster boarding. It's free, but you can only have one FastPASS active at a time.

4 Saving on Admission
Discounted admission tickets for multi-day stays and multi-park visits are usually available and very useful. Check with a travel agent, area hotels, or on the Disneyland® website.

5 Prebooking
Buying your admission tickets in advance saves both time and effort. Try the Disney website or the ticket hotline to book beforehand.

6 Disney Hotels
Staying at one of the three official Disney hotels is not cheap but convenient for access. Disney's Grand Californian *(see p149)* even has a direct entrance to California Adventure.

7 Kids' Matters
Each park has baby care centers and baby stroller rental stations. Some rides have minimum height requirements.

8 What to Wear
Wear comfortable shoes and clothes and bring a sweater or jacket if staying until after dark, even in summer.

9 What to Bring
Bring a hat, sunscreen, extra batteries, and whatever else you need. It's all available in the park, but at inflated prices.

10 Souvenirs
Try not to stock up on souvenirs early in the day to avoid having to carry them around. World of Disney at Downtown Disney® has the best selection.

Shopping center in Downtown Disney®

Call 714-781-4400 for the Disney ticket hotline

Top 10: Disney by Numbers

1. 650 million guests since opening
2. 1.1 million plants planted every year
3. Seven US presidents have visited
4. 1.2 million gallons of soft drinks sold annually
5. 5,000 gallons of paint used each year
6. 800 species of saplings throughout the resort
7. 25,000 employees ("cast members")
8. 4 million hamburgers consumed annually
9. 30 tons of trash collected every day
10. 100,000 light bulbs illuminate the resort

Walt Disney's Vision

Walt Disney (1901–66), the father of Mickey Mouse and other beloved cartoon characters, was a pioneer in the field of animation. A relentlessly driven and inventive man, he wished to share his brilliant imagination with families in a non-cinematic way. Watching his own children at play in an ordinary amusement park, Disney was struck by his ultimate inspiration – he would build a place that was clean and filled with all kinds of attractions that parents and kids could enjoy together. Walt Disney envisioned a theme park revolving around five lands: Main Street, a setting plucked from late-19th-/early 20th-century America; Adventureland, imbued with the mystery of exotic locales; Frontierland, an homage to the pioneers; Fantasyland, a place of whimsy inspired by the song "When you Wish Upon a Star;" and Tomorrowland, with a futuristic theme fit for the budding Space Age. Disney picked a 160-acre site in Anaheim and, like the captain of a great ship, over-saw every aspect of the planning and construction of Disneyland®. When the Magic Kingdom opened its gates in 1955 and 28,000 people stormed in, tears reportedly streamed down Walt Disney's cheeks – his great dream had finally become a reality.

Disneyland® Opening Day

It was impossible to tell from Walt's smile, but opening day at Disneyland® was close to a disaster. Temperatures soared, the parking lot asphalt bubbled, and crowds far exceeded capacity thanks to nearly 22,000 forged tickets. Rides failed, tempers flared, and it was all broadcast live! But the rest, as they say, is history.

Walt Disney with children enjoying a ride in Disneyland®

TOP 10 Catalina Island

This island may be only 22 miles (35 km) across the sea, but it's a world away from the urban velocity of LA. Ferries dock in Mediterranean-flavored Avalon, the island's commercial hub. Most of the interior is a protected nature preserve that may only be explored on foot or bicycle (permit required), or by taking an organized tour. These are excellent ways to learn about the island's colorful history as a destination for sea otter poachers, smugglers, Union soldiers, mining speculators, and finally, tourists.

View of Avalon Harbor

🍽 Armstrong's on the bay is the best place for fresh fish, while Steve's Steakhouse scores high for meat.

⛵ The full Catalina experience should involve the water. Swimming, snorkeling, diving, kayaking, or a glass-bottom boat tour constitute great options.

Catalina is at its most pleasant in the evening after the last ferry has whisked off the day-trippers, so consider an overnight stay.

• Visitor's Bureau: Green Pleasure Pier, 310-510-1520 • Catalina Island Museum: Casino Building, 310-510-2414 • Wrigley Memorial & Botanical Gardens: 1400 Avalon Canyon, 310-510-2595 • Catalina Express: 800-481-3470 • Island Express: 800-228-2566 • Discovery Tours: 888-317-3576 • Catalina Adventure Tours: 562-432-8828 or 877-432-8828

Top 10 Features

1. Avalon Casino
2. Catalina Island Museum
3. Casino Point Marine Park
4. The Tuna Club
5. Green Pleasure Pier
6. Lover's Cove
7. Wrigley Memorial & Botanical Gardens
8. Catalina Country Club
9. Catalina Buffalo
10. Two Harbors

1 Avalon Casino
This Art Deco landmark *(above)*, built for William Wrigley Jr., opened in 1929 and was never a gambling place. It contains a movie theater and a ballroom that once hosted nationally broadcast concerts. Murals of underwater scenes adorn the exterior.

2 Catalina Island Museum
Over 7,000 years of island history come alive at this small museum in the Casino building. Highlights include locally found archaeological artifacts, pottery, and photographs from Catalina's days as the darling of Hollywood.

3 Casino Point Marine Park
Great for encounters with finned creatures, this reserve was Southern California's first city-designed water park (established in 1965). Fun for divers *(below)*.

4 The Tuna Club
The nation's oldest (1898) fishing club, it was the first to develop modern angling rules for sport-fishing. Winston Churchill and Teddy Roosevelt have been visitors here.

➡ *Afishinados (310-510-2440) operates charter fishing trips; you can fish for free from the pier*

5 Green Pleasure Pier

This green pier *(left)* has been the hub of Avalon activity since 1909. For years, it was the official weighing station for tuna, marlin, and sea bass brought in by game fishing enthusiasts.

9 Catalina Buffalo

Island explorations may lead to encounters with herds of chocolate-colored buffalo. The first 14 animals were brought to Catalina in 1924 for a Zane Grey film.

10 Two Harbors

Popular with boaters, hikers, and campers, tiny Two Harbors *(left)* is a slow-paced rustic village on a natural isthmus about 23 miles (37 km) west of Avalon. It is served by ferry from the mainland and by bus from Avalon.

A Wealth of Wildlife

Catalina has a unique ecosystem, including such endemic species as the Channel Island fox and the Catalina ground squirrel. The introduction of non-native animals – such as pigs, goats, deer, and buffalo – resulted in overgrazing, a trend the Catalina Island Conservancy is seeking to reverse. Another wildlife restoration project has returned the California bald eagle to the island's skies. Pelicans, cormorants, and gulls can also be spotted. The ocean waters are abundant with sea lions, Garibaldi, flying fish, and shark.

6 Lover's Cove

Rent a snorkel and take to the clear blue waters of this poetically named marine preserve teeming with golden Garibaldi (California's state marine fish), as well as schools of opaleyes, blue perch, and other fish.

7 Wrigley Memorial & Botanical Gardens

The monument to William Wrigley Jr., built in 1935 with local materials, lords over huge gardens *(right)*. Plants here include eight species unique to the island, including Catalina ironwood and wild tomato.

8 Catalina Country Club

In 1929, William Wrigley Jr. made Catalina the spring training ground for his baseball team. The historic clubhouse is now a restaurant *(above)*.

Left **Donald Douglas, airplane designer** Right **The Los Angeles Riots (1992)**

Moments in History

1781: The Founding of Los Angeles

Under orders of King Carlos III of Spain, the governor of California Felipe de Neve laid out a small settlement along a river valley and, on September 4, called it El Pueblo de la Reina de Los Angeles (The Town of the Queen of the Angels), another name for the Virgin Mary *(see p71)*.

2 1850: LA Becomes a City

After the US-Mexican War ended in 1846–48, Los Angeles became part of the USA on April 4, five months before California became the 31st state. With a tiny population of about 1,600, this unruly and lawless backwater lacked even such basic urban infrastructures as graded roads and street lights.

The founding of Los Angeles

3 1876: The Arrival of the Railroad

Few events have stimulated LA's growth more than its connection to the transcontinental railroad. A small army of Chinese immigrants built the Southern Pacific railroad from Los Angeles to San Francisco. The last spike – made of gold – was driven in ceremoniously on September 5.

4 1911: The Movies Come to LA

British immigrants David and William Horsely founded Hollywood's first permanent movie studio, the Nestor Film Company, in an old tavern at the corner of Sunset Boulevard and Gower Street. Today, the site is occupied by CBS Television. Within a decade, the district had become the world's movie capital and by the 1930s and 1940s, Hollywood had officially entered its "Golden Age."

5 1913: The Opening of the LA Aqueduct

"There it is! Take it!" is how William Mulholland, father of the world's longest aqueduct, famously greeted the first spurt of water to arrive in LA from the Owens Valley, some 250 miles (400 km) north, on November 5. Even today, the Los Angeles aqueduct continues to supply over 75 percent of the water needed by the residents of this metropolis, as it is partly located in a subtropical desert.

For more on historic sites **See p71**

Los Angeles Top 10

6 The 1920s: The Birth of the Aviation Industry

In possession of just $1,000, but driven by a dream, 28-year-old Donald Douglas began designing airplanes in the back of a barber shop. A year later, the first Cloudster cargo plane propelled his Douglas Aircraft Company into prominence. It went on to become one of the world's leading airplane manufacturers.

7 1965: The Watts Riots

The arrest of a young black motorist suspected of drunk driving by white policemen on August 11 sparked off six days of rioting and resulted in 34 deaths, over 1,000 injuries, and $40 million in property damage.

8 1968: The Assassination of Robert F. Kennedy

On June 5, just minutes after wrapping up a speech to celebrate his victory in the California primary, presidential candidate Robert F. Kennedy was brutally gunned down by Sirhan Sirhan.

9 1992: The LA Riots

The city erupted into violence on April 29 after the acquittal of four white police officers on trial for beating up black motorist Rodney King, an incident famously captured on videotape. The toll this time: 55 dead, 2,300 injured, and $785 million in property damage.

10 1994: Northridge Earthquake

Millions were jolted awake on January 17 by a violent earthquake measuring 6.7 on the Richter scale. It caused 57 deaths and 6,500 injuries, interrupting water, electrical, and gas services, and damaging freeways and homes.

Top 10 LA Movers & Shakers

1 Junípero Serra (1713–84)
Spanish missionary and founder of 21 California missions, including LA's Mission San Gabriel.

2 Felipe de Neve (1728–84)
The Spanish governor who founded Los Angeles in 1781.

3 Stephen Watts Kearny (1794–1848)
The American general who assisted in the capture of Los Angeles from the Mexican army in 1847.

4 Phineas Banning (1830–85)
The "Father of Los Angeles Harbor," who also constructed Southern California's first railroad in 1869.

5 William Mulholland (1855–1935)
The chief engineer of Los Angeles's Water Department.

6 Edward Doheny (1856–1935)
This miner turned multi-millionaire discovered oil near downtown LA in 1892.

7 George Freeth (1883–1916)
This Hawaiian-Irish athlete introduced surfing to Southern California in the early 1900s.

8 Harrison Gray Otis (1837–1917)
City booster and publisher of the *Los Angeles Times* for three decades.

9 D.W. Griffith (1875–1948)
Pioneering film-maker and co-founder of United Artists.

10 Tom Bradley (1917–98)
LA's first African-American mayor governed for an unprecedented five terms.

Left **Schindler House** Right **Wayfarer's Chapel**

🔟 Architectural Landmarks

1 The Getty Center
The architecture of the extraordinary Getty Center is said to outshine the art displayed within its galleries. Architect Richard Meier has created an elegant, sophisticated space that is nevertheless warmly welcoming *(see pp12–15)*.

2 The Gamble House
This stunning Pasadena Craftsman bungalow marks the pinnacle of the career of Charles and Henry Greene. Built in 1908 as the retirement home of David and Mary Gamble of the Procter & Gamble family, the house has a beautiful garden, wide terraces, and open sleeping porches *(see p91)*.

3 Schindler House
The private home and studio of Vienna-born architect Rudolf Schindler (1887–1953) is a modern architectural classic. Completed in 1922, the house's flat roof, open floor plan, ample use of glass, and rooms opening to a courtyard greatly influenced California architecture. Today,

it houses the MAK Center for Arts and Architecture that hosts a year-round schedule of tours, exhibitions, lectures, and other interesting events. ✆ *Map M4 • 835 N Kings Rd, West Hollywood • 323-651-1510 • Open 11am–6pm Wed–Sun • Adm*

4 Hollyhock House
One of Frank Lloyd Wright's masterpieces, the 1921 Hollyhock House was the architect's first LA commission. Anchoring Barnsdall Park, the avant-garde architecture of the house takes full advantage of the mild California climate. Wright created seamless transitions between indoor and outdoor space and made ample use of patios, porches, and rooftop terraces *(see p97)*.

5 Wayfarer's Chapel
Lloyd Wright, son of Frank Lloyd Wright, set this unique glass chapel amid a grove of redwood trees on an isolated hilltop overlooking the Pacific on the Palos Verdes peninsula. Today, this fairytale structure is one of the most popular wedding venues in LA *(see p119)*.

6 Chiat/Day Building
Reflecting architect Frank Gehry's sculptural approach to architecture, this 1991 building was commissioned by the advertising firm Chiat/Day as its West Coast corporate headquarters. It has as its center a three-story tall pair of binoculars

The Gamble House

For Downtown architecture See p77

Chiat/Day Building

designed by Claes Oldenburg and Coosje van Bruggen. The pile of angled rust-colored columns on the right resembles a decon-structed forest. ⊗ Map A5 • 340 Main St, Venice • Not open to public

Walt Disney Concert Hall
This Frank Gehry-designed Downtown extravaganza is easily recognized by its shiny and dynamically curved exterior. It is the home of the Los Angeles Philharmonic Orchestra and seats over 2,000 people. The city-block-sized complex also comprises two small outdoor amphitheaters (see p54 & p72).

Chemosphere
John Lautner's bold, often experimental architectural style is perfectly exemplified in this unique private home in the Hollywood Hills. Resembling a flying saucer on a single concrete column, it was built in 1960, the same year President John F. Kennedy launched the challenge to put a man on the moon. The house was featured in Brian de Palma's 1984 movie Body Double. ⊗ Map D2 • 776 Torreyson Dr, Hollywood Hills • Not open to the public

Bradbury Building
The light-flooded atrium of this 1893 office building, with its open-cage elevators, frilly iron work, and marble floors, is one of LA's supreme architectural landmarks. Architect George Wyman allegedly accepted the job only after consulting a Ouija board. Movie buffs might recognize it from Blade Runner and Chinatown.

Cathedral of Our Lady of the Angels
Behind the fortress-like exterior of the cathedral, designed by José Rafael Moneo, awaits a minimalist hall of worship where the lack of right angles and supporting pillars creates a sense of spacious loftiness. You don't have to be a Roman Catholic to appreciate the lovely tapestries of the nave, depicting dozens of saints (see p72).

Bradbury Building

Left **Huntington Botanical Gardens** Center **Greystone Park** Right **Wrigley Mansion & Gardens**

🔟 Parks & Gardens

1 Huntington Library, Art Collections, & Botanical Gardens

A perfect synthesis of nature and culture, this amazing estate houses priceless collections of paintings and rare manuscripts that were started by railroad tycoon Henry E. Huntington and his wife, Arabella, in the early 19th century (see pp22–5).

2 Griffith Park

The country's largest urban park (see pp28–9) is filled with museums, entertainment opportunities for children, hiking and horse trails, and the famous Griffith Park Observatory.

3 Greystone Park & Mansion

Popular with wedding planners and visitors in search of solitude, this secluded park affords great views of Beverly Hills. Its centerpiece is a 55-room mansion built in 1928 by oil tycoon Edward Doheny as a wedding present for his son Ned. The estate has been featured in many films, including Air Force One.
◈ Map J3 • 905 Loma Vista Dr, Beverly Hills • 310-285-6830 • Open most days; call for park hours. Mansion open for special events only • Free • www.greystonemansion.org

4 Virginia Robinson Gardens

The 1911 estate of department-store heiress Virginia Robinson is one of the oldest in Beverly Hills. Stroll in gardens with fountains and statuettes past towering king palms and elegant camellias flourishing in this quiet hideaway.
◈ Map J4 • 1008 Elden Way • 310-550-2065 • Tours: 10am & 1pm Tue–Fri by appt only • Adm • www.robinsongardens.org

5 Exposition Park Rose Garden

This lovely rose garden dates back to 1928 and features about 15,000 rose bushes in bloom from March to November. Great for picnics or for a respite from museum-hopping. ◈ Map D3 • 701 State Dr • 9am–sunset daily (closed Jan 1–Mar 15) • Free • www.laparks.org/exporosegarden/rosegarden.htm

6 Wrigley Mansion & Gardens

The winter home of William Wrigley Jr. (of Wrigley's chewing gum fame) is backed by a lovely green rose garden and now serves as the headquarters of the Pasadena Tournament of Roses Association (see p88).

Virginia Robinson Gardens

For more information on LA parks, log on to www.laparks.org

Palisades Park

with 70 sculptures by some of the greatest 19th- and 20th-century European and American artists, Auguste Rodin and Alexander Calder among them. ⊗ *Map C2 • UCLA campus, Westwood • Open any time • Free • www.hammer. ucla.edu/collections/detail/collection_id/6*

Runyon Canyon Park
Minutes from the Walk of Fame, this small urban park has some moderately difficult trails and a colorful history – the ruins near the Fuller Steet entrance were built in 1930 by opera star John McCormack and Errol Flynn lived in one of the pool houses in the late 1950s. The Santa Monica Mountains Conservancy purchased the park in 1983. ⊗ *Map N1 • At the end of Fuller St off Franklin Ave • 323-666-5046 • Open until sunset (avoid after dark)*

Self-Realization Fellowship Lake Shrine
Bathed in an ambience of beauty and serenity, this hidden sanctuary was created in 1950 by Parama-hansa Yogananda, an Indian-born spiritual leader. Wander over to the shrine to Mahatma Gandhi or the spring-fed lake, meditate inside a recreated 16th-century windmill, or study the Court of Religions that honors all of the world's major religions. ⊗ *Map B3 • 17190 Sunset Blvd • 310-454-4114 • Open 9am–4:30pm Tue–Sat, noon–4:30pm Sun • Free • www.lakeshrine.org*

Palisades Park
Famous for its swaying palm trees and picture-perfect views of Santa Monica Bay (especially at sunset), Palisades Park is a playground for young and old, locals and visitors, families and courting couples. Stretching for 13 blocks atop a bluff overlooking the ocean, its benches and lawns invite picnics and people-watching. A nostalgic curiosity is the Camera Obscura inside a seniors' center. ⊗ *Map C3 • Ocean Ave between Santa Monica Pier & San Vincente Blvd • Open any time • Free*

Franklin D. Murphy Sculpture Garden
Tucked away in the northeastern corner of the UCLA campus, this delightful little oasis is dotted

Left & Right **Venice Beach**

🔟 Beaches

1 Nicholas Canyon Beach

This 2-mile (3-km) lovely beach is a secret even from locals, because of its isolation and distance from the city. It hugs the base of a bluff and is a great place for those seeking solitude. Work on the tan, or sit watching the waves kiss the sand. ⊗ *33900 block of Pacific Coast Hwy, near Ventura County Line*

2 El Matador Beach

Rugged, secluded, and dotted with large boulders artistically eroded by nature, this small cliff-backed beach is one of LA's finest. Its remoteness, limited parking, and cumbersome access via a gravelly trail keep the crowds at bay. There are no facilities available, but you can explore tide pools and caves, or take a dip. Nude sunbathing is illegal in L.A. County but some does occur. ⊗ *32900 block of Pacific Coast Hwy, Malibu*

3 Zuma Beach

This 2-mile (3-km) ribbon of fine, sparkling sand is one of LA's most popular beaches. Its clean water and mostly mid-sized waves are great for sports such as bodysurfing, boogie-boarding, and swimming. It teems with families and hormone-crazed teenagers on sunny summer Sundays but is nearly deserted the rest of the week, making it perfect for quiet picnics and extended walks along the beach. ⊗ *30000 block of Pacific Coast Hwy, Malibu*

4 Malibu Lagoon State/Surfrider Beach

Wedged in between the Malibu Pier and the Malibu Colony gated celebrity enclave, this popular beach offers many diversions. Watch surfers shred the waves at Surfrider Beach. The eponymous lagoon is a major stopover for migratory birds, while the nearby Adamson House with its idyllic gardens overlooks Malibu Pier and Malibu Lagoon. The house showcases pretty ceramic tiles *(see p117)*. ⊗ *Map A3 • 23200 block of Pacific Coast Hwy, Malibu*

5 Santa Monica Beach

This easy-to-access beach is one of LA's busiest. Families love the Santa Monica Pier *(see p51 & p117)* with its pretty historical carousel and amusement park. Fitness buffs can get their kicks from pedaling or skating down a paved path running past the restored Muscle Beach, the birth-place of the Southern California exercise craze back in the 1930s. ⊗ *Map C3 • Along Pacific Coast Hwy in Santa Monica*

Santa Monica Beach

➜ *Beaches are open 7am–10pm. For recorded coastal weather forecast, call 310-457-9701*

Manhattan Beach

Venice Beach
The beach itself plays second fiddle to Venice's outlandish Ocean Front Walk, which is a magnet for eccentrics and those who love watching them. Against a backdrop of trinket shops and cafés, your encounters may include chainsaw jugglers, hulky musclemen, or even a singing Sikh on roller-blades *(see p118)*. ✍ *Map C3 • Ocean Front Walk between Venice Blvd & Rose Ave*

Manhattan Beach
The Beach Boys, who grew up around here, found inspiration for their inimitable surf music in the white sands and glorious waves of this upscale yet relaxed seaside town. Longboarders still compete for the perfect ride, especially in the area around the Manhattan Pier, which is home to an aquarium *(see p118)*. ✍ *Map C4 • West of Highland Ave*

Hermosa Beach
South of Manhattan Beach, Hermosa *(see p119)* has a busy bar and restaurant scene right where Pier Avenue meets the sand. Beach volleyball is the local pastime and national tournaments take place throughout the year. Only the paved South Bay Bicycle Trail that runs

from Marina del Rey to Palos Verdes lies between the sand and private homes. ✍ *Map C5 • Around Pier Ave*

Cabrillo Beach
The colorful sails of windsurfers flutter like giant butterflies along this beach on the breakwater of LA Harbor. Visit the nearby Cabrillo Marine Aquarium *(see p127)* to learn about marine life. ✍ *Map D6 • Stephen M. White Dr, San Pedro*

Seal Beach
Head to this low-key ocean playground just south of the San Gabriel River for a taste of small-town America. Warm waters and small to mid-size waves make it ideal for swimmers and surfers. A 1,865-ft (600-m) pier with a diner anchors Seal Beach. ✍ *Map F6 • Along Ocean Ave, Orange County*

Note: *Alcohol is not permitted on L.A. County beaches and fires are only allowed at Dockweiler, Cabrillo and Mother's beaches*

Left **Rose Bowl** Right **Hollywood Park Racetrack**

🔟 Sports & Fitness Venues

1 Rose Bowl
Every New Year's Day since 1923, the classic stand-off between the leading teams of college football's Pacific Coast and Big Ten conferences has taken place at this historic landmark stadium *(see p88)*. The Bowl has also hosted five professional football Super Bowls, the 1994 World Cup soccer finals, and many other major sporting events. Its giant flea market, held every second Sunday of the month, is legendary.

2 Dodger Stadium
Dodger Stadium, home of the LA Dodgers major league baseball team, is widely regarded as a crown jewel among American ballparks. Completed in 1962, its clever configuration allows for good sight lines from all 56,000 seats. Panoramic city and mountain views are an extra bonus. Guided tours, which include peeks at the press box and dugout, are offered on non-game days *(see p81)*.

3 Staples Center
This modern temple to professional team sports is home base for basketball's Lakers, Clippers, and Sparks, and ice hockey's Kings. Staples Center is also a preferred stop for blockbuster music acts à la Barbra Streisand, Jay-Z, Katy Perry, and the Rolling Stones. Thanks to steep bleachers, views are great from most seats. 🚭 *Map S6 • 1111 S Figueroa St, Downtown • 213-742-7340 • www.staplescenter.com*

4 Santa Anita Racetrack
One of the most celebrated thoroughbred racetracks in the US, Santa Anita opened in 1934 and has been a hit with Hollywood stars and the LA elite ever since. The season runs from December 26 to April. 🚭 *Map F1 • 285 W Huntington Dr, Arcadia • 626-574-7223 • www.santaanita.com*

5 Hollywood Park Racetrack
Nicknamed the "Track of Lakes and Flowers," Hollywood Park has seen its share of triumphs since it opened in 1938. Founded by the Hollywood Turf Club under its chairman, movie mogul Jack Warner, it counted Bing Crosby and Walt Disney among its original shareholders. Thoroughbred races take place from late April to late July and again from early November to December. 🚭 *Map D4 • 1050 S Prairie Ave, Inglewood • 310-419-1500*

Staples Center

For beaches and watersports See pp44–5

Los Angeles Memorial Coliseum

6 Los Angeles Memorial Coliseum & Sports Arena

An architectural triumph when completed in 1923, the Coliseum *(see p83)* in Exposition Park is now a National Historic Landmark. It first rose to prominence as a key site of the 1932 Summer Olympics and has also hosted the 1984 Games, two Super Bowls, and one World Series. Pope John Paul II has been cheered on here. ✆ *Map D3 • 3911 South Figueroa St, Exposition Park • 213-747-7111 • www. lacoliseumlive.com*

Sign for Crunch Gym

7 StubHub Center

At the core of LA's modern sports complex is a 27,000-seat soccer stadium. It is the home turf of the Los Angeles Galaxy and Chivas USA, both Major League Soccer (MLS) teams, and also serves as the US men's and women's national soccer teams' training headquarters. ✆ *Map E5 • 18400 Avalon Blvd, Cal State Dominguez Hills campus, Carson • 310-630-2000 • www.stubhubcenter.com*

8 Yoga Works

This yoga studio offers several classes in nine locations and caters for all levels. If you don't know your downward-facing dog from your sun salutation, take an introductory class to learn about basic postures and breathing techniques. ✆ *Map A4 • 2215 Main St (also at 1426 Montana Ave), Santa Monica • 310-664-6470 • www.yogaworks.com*

9 Crunch Gym

Vanity rules at this state-of-the-art gym famous for its celebrity clientele and innovative workout classes. Get killer abs and buns of steel while sweating through unusual offerings such as Cardio Striptease, Kama Sutra Yoga, or Pole Dancing. Finish up with a relaxing session in the sauna or steam room. ✆ *Map M3 • 8000 Sunset Blvd • 323-654-4550 • www.crunch.com*

10 Gold's Gym

Steel your biceps and other body parts in the hallowed halls once haunted by Mr. Universe himself, Arnold "The Terminator" Schwarzenegger. Other celebrity members have included Mel Gibson, Jodie Foster, and Keanu Reeves. Day passes are available. ✆ *Map Q3 • 360 Hampton Dr, Venice • 310-392-6004 • www.goldsgym.com*

47

Nixon Presidential Library & Museum

⭑10 Drives & Day Trips

1 Mission San Fernando Rey de España

The 17th of the 21 missions founded by Franciscans in California, San Fernando was established in 1797 to supply food for El Pueblo de Los Angeles. The mission church is an exact replica of the original, destroyed in the 1971 Sylmar earthquake. The adjacent *convento* (living quarters) is the state's largest surviving adobe structure. ⌾ *15151 San Fernando Mission Blvd, Mission Hills • 818-361-0186 • Open 9am–4:30pm daily • Adm*

Mission San Fernando Rey de España

2 Mission San Gabriel Arcangel

Heavy flooding forced the fourth of the California missions to relocate to this spot only five years after it was founded in 1771. Though struck twice by earthquakes, the mission prospered with the help of Indian converts, many of whom are buried here. The grounds are peppered with fountains and fireplaces. A small museum has other exhibits. ⌾ *Map E2 • 428 S Mission Dr, San Gabriel • 626-457-3035 • Open 9am–4:30pm daily • Adm*

3 Mulholland Drive

Named after William Mulholland, the architect of the Los Angeles aqueduct, this quintessential LA road winds for about 25 miles (40 km) along a Santa Monica Mountains ridge from Hollywood to the western San Fernando Valley. On clear days, the panoramic views are truly stunning. ⌾ *Map B2*

4 Watts Towers

This folk art masterpiece is a whimsical trio of spires, adorned with rainbow-colored pieces of tile, glass, pottery, shells, and other scavenged materials. The sculpture, completed in 1954, represents the life's work of Italian immigrant Simon Rodia. Located in a high-crime neighborhood, avoid after dark. ⌾ *Map E4 • 1765 E 107th St, Watts • 213-847-4646 • Call for opening hours • Adm • www.wattstowers.org*

5 Six Flags Magic Mountain

The Holy Grail for roller coaster junkies, Six Flags has more ways to catapult, spin, loop, spiral, and twist than you or your stomach can imagine. Favorite white-knuckle rides include X, the world's first four-dimensional coaster, and Superman: The Escape, which has you free-falling for 6.5 seconds. ⌾ *26101 Magic Mountain Parkway, Valencia • 661-255-4104 • Open late Mar– early Sep: 12:30–6pm daily; rest of the year: weekends & hols • Adm • www.sixflags.com*

6 Santa Barbara & Wine Country

This graceful "Mediterranean" town with its Spanish-style architecture and villa-studded hillsides is imbued with an unpretentious charm. With a stately mission and historical adobes, it is also a must visit for wine connoisseurs. Head for the tasting rooms of the wine country around Santa Ynez, a 45-minute drive away. ⊗ *On Hwy 101, about 90 miles (145 km) north of LA*

7 Ventura & Channel Islands National Park

Ventura's revitalized Main Street is a fun place to browse through antiques and second-hand stores and for a look inside the Mission San Buenaventura. The town is the gateway to the magnificent Channel Islands National Park. Boat excursions to the islands leave from Ventura Harbor year-round. ⊗ *On Hwy 101, about 65 miles (105 km) north of LA*

8 Laguna Beach

The picturesque setting of this friendly seaside resort has captivated artists for over a century. In summer, Laguna hosts three major art festivals, including the Pageant of the

Mission San Buenaventura church, Ventura

Recreated Oval Office, Ronald Reagan Library

Masters, which recreates well-known paintings as living tableaux using a cast of costumed locals. The Laguna Art Museum showcases vintage and contemporary California landscapes. ⊗ *On Hwy 1, about 60 miles (97 km) south of LA*

9 Nixon Presidential Library & Museum

This memorial to the 37th US president (1913–94) includes a museum, gardens, and the restored 1910 farmhouse where he was born. High-tech exhibits focus on Nixon's achievements, but also include a gallery about Watergate. A recreation of the Lincoln Sitting Room, Nixon's favorite in the White House, is another highlight. ⊗ *18001 Yorba Linda Blvd, Yorba Linda • 714-993-3393 • Open 10am–5pm daily (from 11am Sun) • Adm • www.nixonlibrary.gov*

10 Ronald Reagan Presidential Library & Museum

A chunk of the Berlin Wall, a cruise missile, and a recreated Oval Office are the highlights of this museum devoted to the 40th US president (1911–2004). Exhibits trace Reagan's life from his childhood, through his Hollywood career to his political ascent, first as California governor, then as president. ⊗ *40 Presidential Dr, Simi Valley • 800-410-8354 • Open 10am–5pm daily • Adm • www.reaganlibrary.net*

Left **California Science Center** Center **Natural History Museum** Right **Los Angeles Zoo**

🔟 LA for Children

1 Universal Studios Hollywood℠

This theme park attached to the world's largest movie studio is LA's biggest tourist attraction. A ticket buys a day of thrill rides and live action shows, and includes encounters with Spider-Man, the Transformers, Shrek, King Kong, and other movie icons. A must-do is the narrated tram tour to the backlot with its famous outdoor sets *(see pp26–7)*.

Shrek, Universal Studios Hollywood℠

2 Disneyland®

Over half a century after it first opened its doors, the "Magic Kingdom" continues to be right on top of most children's must-see lists. A one-, two-, or three-day visit is guaranteed to delight, amaze, and exhaust the kids, especially since expansions have added a second theme park, Disney's California Adventure™, and the Downtown Disney® entertainment district to Disneyland® *(see pp30–35)*.

3 California Science Center

Located in Exposition Park, this interactive museum makes learning about science and technology a fun experience. Feel a simulated earthquake, watch chickens hatch out of eggs, design your own car, and marvel at the inner workings of a 50-ft (15-m) long robotic doll named Tess. The adjoining Air and Space Gallery in a separate building teaches the principles of flight and space exploration *(see p81)*.

4 Natural History Museum

This engaging museum pays homage to the entire animal kingdom, including extinct species such as the perennially popular dinosaurs. Special child-oriented facilities include the Discovery Center stocked with puppets, storybooks, and a fossil-rubbing station; and the Insect Zoo, home to a host of creepy crawlies, creatures as diverse as tarantulas, centipedes, and ants *(see p81)*.

5 Long Beach Aquarium of the Pacific

Take a virtual dive through three major regions of the Pacific Ocean at this first-rate aquarium. You'll travel to the kelp beds of Southern and Baja California, the stormy shores of the northern Pacific, and the coral reefs of the tropical Pacific. Pick up laminated "dive charts" to help you identify the species, then meet some of them in the flesh *(see p128)*.

Los Angeles Zoo

6 Kids love the Elephants of Asia exhibit and the Winnick Family Children's Zoo, located within the LA Zoo. Pet barnyard animals at Muriel's Ranch, greet the zoo's newest members in the animal nursery, and dress up for interactive play and storytelling at the Adventure Theater.
◈ Map D1 • 5333 Zoo Drive • Open 10am–5pm daily • Closed 25 Dec • Adm (free for under 2s) • www.lazoo.org

Cabrillo Marine Aquarium

7 Though small, this facility offers an entertaining introduction to life in Southern California's ocean waters. The playful yet educational exhibits are ideal for children. The staff also organizes various activities, including guided tide pool walks, a marine laboratory workshop, and even "sleepovers with the fishes," when kids can "camp" out in the aquarium under staff supervision (see p127).

Storyopolis

8 Creativity is king at this "city of stories." Its shelves bulge with some 5,000 kiddie books, while its walls showcase the work of top illustrators. The store is also known for its family events and storytelling sessions.
◈ Map C1 • 16740 Ventura Blvd, Studio City • 818-990-7600 • Open 11am–5pm Mon–Sat (to 4pm Sun) • Free • www.storyopolis.com

Bob Baker Marionette Theater

9 A show at this landmark theater, founded in 1963, is truly a treat. Seated on a fluffy carpet, children watch in

Entrance to the Santa Monica Pier

wonder as the cast of marionettes and puppets sing and dance before their eyes, sometimes even interacting with them. All characters are made in the on-site workshop and many are for sale, so you can take some home with you. ◈ Map T3 • 1345 W 1st St • 213-250-9995 • Shows: 10:30am Tue–Fri, 2:30pm Sat & Sun (reservations required) • Adm • www.bobbakermarionettes.com

Santa Monica Pier

10 Pet a sea cucumber, take to the skies in a Ferris wheel, or watch local fisherfolk reel in their latest catch at this pier. These are just some of the activities on California's oldest amusement pier, whose attractions draw over three million people a year. During summer, be sure to make it to the popular free concert series that takes place on Thursday nights (see p117).

Left **Rodeo Drive** Right **Melrose Avenue**

Shopping Streets

Main Street, Santa Monica
A laid-back yet sophisticated string of one-of-a-kind boutiques (with the occasional chain store thrown in for good measure), Main Street makes for a fun and eclectic shopping experience with plenty of cafés for people-watching. On Sundays, catch the farmers market (see p123).

Montana Avenue
You're likely to bump into celebrities in the upscale boutiques on Montana Avenue. It's fun peeking at the clothes, home furnishings, beauty products, and exercise gear favored by fashionistas. ⊗ Map C3 • Between 7th & 17th Sts, Santa Monica

Robertson Boulevard
Price tags are steep at the boutiques on this ultra-cool two-block stretch, but you may be browsing next to celebrities such as Cameron Diaz or Jennifer Aniston. Part of the mix are cutting-edge LA designers. ⊗ Map L5 • Between 3rd St & Beverly Blvd

Rodeo Drive
A stroll along this fabled shopping street (see p111 & p114) is a must. All the big names in haute couture have staked out their turf on Rodeo, including Armani, Chanel, Ralph Lauren, and Versace. For better prices, walk one block east to Beverly Drive.

Melrose Avenue
Melrose puts the "fun" into "funky" (see p104 & p108). Tattooed 20-somethings pick up vintage clothing, eccentric clubwear, and jewelry in stores between La Brea Boulevard and Fairfax Avenue. West of Fairfax is a newer designer enclave and farther west, the Pacific Design Center (see p103) is more about trendy home furnishings.

Abbot Kinney Boulevard
The pint-sized stores here teem with character, not to mention characters. This is Venice, after all: laid-back, hip, and plenty artistic. Fans of 1950s furniture, New Agers in search of aura-enhancing elixirs, and gift shoppers will find all that they want. Fairly moderate prices. ⊗ Map A6 • Between Venice Blvd & Main St

Third Street Promenade
A carnival atmosphere reigns on this popular pedestrian-only strip, especially in summer.

Main Street, Santa Monica

Third Street Promenade

Upscale chains such as Fred Segal and Anthropologie dominate, with a few bookstores and old-timers such as the Puzzle Zoo toy store thrown in *(see pp117–18)*.

8 West Third Street
Wedged in between the Beverly Center and the Original Farmers Market, this mile-long strip is one of the hippest shopping scenes in LA. The bounty ranges from gift stores such as Raena to LA-made fashions at Nathalie Seaver Boutique and international beauty products at Palmetto. ⊗ *Map M5 • Between La Cienega Blvd & Fairfax Ave, W Hollywood*

9 Santee Alley
Bargain hunters will love this pedestrian-only lane, the busiest in the Fashion District and the center of LA's garment industry. In a setting reminiscent of an Oriental bazaar, vendors hawk cut-rate clothing, accessories, and luggage. Alas, name-brand knock-offs are not uncommon, so beware. ⊗ *Map T6 • Between Olympic Blvd & 12th St, Downtown*

10 Old Town Pasadena
Once an ancient crumbling historic district, Old Town Pasadena was given a makeover in the 1990s. Today, Colorado Boulevard and its side streets offer a pleasant shopping experience in mostly mid-priced chains and specialty stores *(see p87)*.

Top 10 Shopping Malls

1 The Grove at Farmers Market
Outdoor mall with mock streetscape and fountains *(see p103)*. ⊗ 323-900-8000

2 Beverly Center
Upscale retail assortment within a fortress-like façade. ⊗ Map L5 • 310-854-0070

3 Santa Monica Place
Frank Gehry-designed mall with great food courts. ⊗ Map A4 • 310-394-5451

4 Glendale Galleria
Dedicated mall-crawlers will love this heaven of over 250 mostly mid-priced stores. ⊗ Map E1 • 818-240-9481

5 Westside Pavilion
Neighborhood mall with the state-of-the-art Landmark Film Center for independent films. ⊗ Map C3 • 310-474-6255

6 Westfield Shoppingtown Century City
Elegant shopping area with boutiques and valet parking. ⊗ Map C2 • 310-553-5300

7 Paseo Colorado
Trendy Pasadena "urban village" with 65 stores and Mediterranean architecture. ⊗ Map F1 • 626-795-8891

8 Hollywood & Highland
Shop beneath the Hollywood Sign at this fanciful outdoor mall in Tinseltown. ⊗ Map P2 • 323-467-6412

9 Westfield Shoppingtown Fashion Square
Indoor mall that prides itself on outstanding service. ⊗ Map C1 • 818-783-0550

10 7th+Fig
Fun architecture, great food, and a colorful farmers market on Thursdays. ⊗ Map T5 • 213-955-7150

 The Wine Merchant's cellars (310-278-7322) in Beverly Hills are superb for top-quality wines

Left **Music Center** Center **Pantages Theatre** Right **Greek Theatre**

🔟 Performing Arts Venues

1 Hollywood Bowl
Concerts beneath the stars at this natural amphitheater are a beloved summer tradition. The range extends from Beethoven to the Beatles, cabaret to rock. Enjoy a picnic before the show. Cheap tickets are available for some shows *(see p95)*.

2 Music Center
This three-venue arts center represents LA culture. The LA Opera, directed by Plàcido Domingo, makes its home at the Dorothy Chandler Pavilion, while cutting-edge plays are presented at the Ahmanson Theater and the Mark Taper Forum. ⊗ *Map V4 • 135 N Grand Ave, Downtown • 213-972-7211*

3 Walt Disney Concert Hall
This Frank Gehry creation, the newest part of the Music Center, features cleverly designed seating which makes listening to the LA Philharmonic Orchestra, playing beneath the sail-like ceiling of the hall, an unforgettable experience *(see p41 & p72)*.

4 Ford Amphitheatre
Built in 1920 and embraced by the Hollywood Hills, this intimate outdoor amphitheater presents a multicultural program of music, dance, film, and theater events. ⊗ *Map P1 • 2580 Cahuenga Blvd E • 323-461-3673 • www.fordtheatres.org*

5 Greek Theatre
Tucked into a hillside in Griffith Park, the popular Greek Theatre *(see p28)* has featured such musical greats as B.B. King. Stars leave their handprints on the Wall of Fame. ⊗ *Map D2 • 2700 N Vermont Ave • 323-665-5857 • www.greektheatrela.com*

6 Gibson Amphitheatre
Next to Universal Studios and Universal CityWalk, this state-of-the-art indoor music venue draws up to 6,300 people with a star-studded calendar of events that have included Fleetwood Mac and Sheryl Crow. ⊗ *Map D2 • 100 Universal City Plaza, Universal City • 818-622-4440 (box office)*

Hollywood Bowl

For the latest information, log on to www.musiccenter.org (Music Center)

Royce Hall, UCLA

7 Pantages Theatre
This Art Deco jewel *(see p11)* has been restored to its 1929 glory. Once a movie palace, its eye-popping auditorium hosted the Academy Awards from 1949–59. ⊛ Map Q2 • 6233 Hollywood Blvd • 323-468-1770 • www.hollywoodpantages.com

8 Dolby Theatre
Home of the Academy Awards since 2002, this is a stunning live entertainment venue with a five-level lobby and a grand spiral staircase. Dolby 3D video imaging and advanced audio technology add to the ambience. ⊛ Map P2 • 6801 Hollywood Blvd • 323-308-6300 • Half-hourly tours: 10:30am–4pm daily • Adm • www.dolbytheatre.com

9 Royce Hall
One of UCLA's original buildings, the 1929 Romanesque Royce Hall *(see p112)* once hosted greats such as George Gershwin. Today, the hall presents an avant-garde calendar of dance, music, and theater events. ⊛ Map C2 • UCLA Campus, Westwood • 310-825-2101 • www.cap.ucla.edu

10 Theatricum Botanicum
This lovely venue was the brainchild of Will Geer, best known for his portrayal of Grandpa in the 1970s TV series *The Waltons*. Watch popular classics. ⊛ Map B2 • 1419 N Topanga Canyon Blvd • 310-455-3723 • www.theatricum.com

Top 10 Comedy Clubs

1 The Laugh Factory
Features big name acts and promising newcomers of all ethnic backgrounds. ⊛ 8001 Sunset Blvd • 323-656-1336

2 The Groundlings
TV star Lisa Kudrow (of the TV series *Friends*) graduated from here. ⊛ 7307 Melrose Ave • 323-934-4747

3 The Improv
Robin Williams has tickled funny bones at this famous haunt with an eatery. ⊛ 8162 Melrose Ave • 323-651-2583

4 Improv Olympic West
LA branch of the famous Chicago original. ⊛ 6366 Hollywood Blvd • 323-962-7560

5 Comedy Store
Legendary club, launched the careers of Jim Carrey and Michael Keaton. ⊛ 8433 Sunset Blvd • 323-650-6268

6 Bang Improv Studios
Veteran improv actors perform low-cost, high-energy shows in a tiny space with flamboyant decor. ⊛ 457 N Fairfax Blvd • 323-653-6886

7 ACME Comedy Theater
Presents the best troupe for sketch comedy in LA in its own theater. ⊛ 135 N La Brea Ave • 323-525-0202

8 The Comedy & Magic Club
Famous comics including Jay Leno (on most Sundays) try out new material here. ⊛ 1018 Hermosa Ave, Hermosa Beach • 310-372-1193

9 The Ice House
One of the US's oldest comedy clubs. ⊛ 24 N Mentor Ave, Pasadena • 626-577-1894

10 HaHa Café
This club nurtures budding comics. ⊛ 5010 Lankershim Blvd • 818-508-4995

A great source of discounted tickets (but available only on the day of the performance) is Theatre In LA **See p140**

Left **ArcLight Cinemas & Cinerama Dome** Right **El Capitan Theatre**

🔟 Movie Theaters

Pacific Theatres at The Grove

1 Pacific Theatres at The Grove
State-of-the-art meets Art Deco charm at this 14-screen complex that evokes the grand theaters of early Los Angeles. Great for star sightings. ✆ *Map N5 • 189 The Grove Drive, Midtown • 323-692-0164*

2 The Bridge
This cutting-edge theater has been subtitled "cinema de lux" for very good reason. Enjoy recently released movies sitting in large and luxurious leather chairs. ✆ *Map D3 • 6081 Center Dr, off Fwy 405 • 310-568-3375*

3 ArcLight Cinemas & Cinerama Dome
The exquisite 14-screen ArcLight is the shiny neighbor of the futuristic Cinerama Dome *(see p96)*. The lobby, lorded over by a giant digital board, leads to a lively café-bar with terrace. Good for star sightings. ✆ *Map Q3 • 6360 W Sunset Blvd • 323-464-4226*

4 El Capitan Theatre
Old-time Hollywood glamour has returned to LA courtesy of the Walt Disney Corporation, which restored this 1926 theater *(see p11)*. It functions as a first-run cinema showing Disney flicks, sometimes preceded by lavish live shows. ✆ *Map P2 • 6838 Hollywood Blvd • 323-467-7674*

5 TCL Chinese Theatre
This flashy 1927 Chinese fantasy palace *(see p11)* is still the site of movie premieres. Catch a blockbuster here – you never know which famous name might be sitting next to you. Note that the sixplex next door to the theater has none of the original's historic flair. ✆ *Map P2 • 6925 Hollywood Blvd • 323-464-6266*

6 The Egyptian Theatre
This oldest of Hollywood Boulevard's themed 1920s movie palaces *(see p11)* houses the American Cinematheque. It presents art house fare and the documentary *Forever Hollywood* on weekends. Regular events feature famous directors and actors. ✆ *Map P2 • 6712 Hollywood Blvd • 323-466-3456*

TCL Chinese Theatre

7 Silent Movie Theatre
The movies of Charlie Chaplin, Rudolph Valentino, and other

silent-era legends regularly reel off at the nation's only remaining silent-movie theater. Live music from the 1920s and classic cartoons often precede screenings. ⊗ Map M4 • 611 N Fairfax Ave, Midtown • 323-655-2510 • www.cinefamily.org

The Nuart Theatre
One of Los Angeles's finest independent theaters shows the kind of experimental and foreign fare that most multiplexes would avoid. The cult classic *The Rocky Horror Picture Show* still runs every Saturday. ⊗ Map C3 • 11272 Santa Monica Blvd • 310-281-8223 • www.landmarktheaters.com

Bing Theater at LACMA
LA's famous art museum *(see pp16–19)* presents high-brow retrospectives of a particular actor or director in its on-site theater with a top-notch digital sound system. On Tuesdays at 1pm, catch classic films for a small fee. ⊗ Map N6 • 5905 Wilshire Blvd, Midtown • 323-857-6010 • www.lacma.org

California Science Center IMAX Theater
IMAX stands for "maximum image" and with a screen that is seven stories tall and 90-ft (27-m) wide, it's a fitting name. The giant screen has a six-channel surround-sound system and ensures total sensorial immersion *(see p81).* ⊗ Map D3 • 700 Exposition Park Dr • 323-744-7400 • www.californiasciencecenter.org

California Science Center

Top 10 Oscar Facts

1 How the Oscar got its Name
The statuette got its name in 1931 after future Academy executive director Margaret Herrick remarked that it resembled her uncle Oscar.

2 Oscar by Numbers
The 13.5-in (34-cm) tall, 8.5-lb (3.8-kg) Oscar has been handed out over 2,800 times.

3 Top Four Oscar-winning Films
Ben Hur, Titanic, and *Lord of the Rings, Return of the King* gained 11 awards each. *West Side Story* received ten.

4 Actor with Most Oscars
A tie – both Walter Brennan and Jack Nicholson won three times.

5 Actress with Most Oscars
Katherine Hepburn, who won the Oscar four times.

6 All-time Oscar Winner
Walt Disney – 26 awards.

7 Youngest Oscar Winner
Shirley Temple, who was six years and 310 days old.

8 Oscar Controversy
In 1972, Marlon Brando refused the Best Actor award in protest against the US government's mistreatment of Native Americans.

9 Oscar Venues
The Hollywood Roosevelt Hotel, Ambassador Hotel, Shrine Auditorium, Pantages Theatre, and The Dolby (current) are the famous ones.

10 Oscar Parties
The official post-award Governor's Ball held at many venues since 1957, moved to the Hollywood and Highland Grand Ballroom in 2002.

For more on Hollywood See pp10–11 & pp58–9

Left **Sony Pictures Studio** Right **Sam French Theatre & Film Bookshop**

Hollywood Connections

1 Warner Bros Tour
This excellent two-hour tour provides a thorough look at both the glamorous history as well as the day-to-day working reality of a major motion picture studio. Watch an introductory movie, visit the museum, and outdoor sets. Actual tour routes depend on that day's production schedule.
◈ Map D1 • 3400 Riverside Dr, Burbank • 818-846-1403 • Adm • http://vipstudiotour.warnerbros.com

2 Sony Pictures Studio Tour
This giant movie lot was the historic home of the famous MGM, producer of well-known classics such as *The Wizard of Oz*, until purchased by Sony in 1990. The two-hour walking tour may include visits to the set of the game show *Jeopardy*, the wardrobe department, and an exciting trip to the sound studio.
◈ Map C3 • 10202 W Washington Blvd, Culver City • 310-244-8687 • Tours: Call for schedule, reservations required • Adm

3 TMZ Hollywood Tour
This two-hour, open-air bus tour is run by the TV show, TMZ. It features guides poised to spot celebrities and interview them on the street. An edgy, fast look at current hot star hang-outs.
◈ Map P2 • 6925 Hollywood Blvd • 855-486-9868 • Tours: Check website for timings • Adm • www.tmz.com/tour

4 Audiences Unlimited
A great way to see stars live is to be part of a studio audience. This organization handles the distribution of free tickets to live tapings, primarily of game shows and sitcoms. Book early for the best selection. Tickets are available online 30 days before show dates. ◈ www.tvtickets.com

5 Larry Edmunds Bookshop
Books about animation, acting, and Hollywood history – Larry Edmunds' fabulous store has it all, as well as historic movie posters, publicity stills,

Warner Bros Studio, Burbank

For information on Hollywood, drop by the Hollywood Visitors' Information Center at Hollywood & Highland Mall See p10 and screenplays. ⌾ Map P2 • 6644 Hollywood Blvd • 323-463-3273 • www. larryedmunds.com

6 Samuel French Theatre & Film Bookshop

This purveyor of printed Hollywood material is geared to the needs of professional actors and screenwriters. The company also publishes and leases scripts of live plays. ⌾ Map N3 • 7623 Sunset Blvd • 866-598-8449 • www.samuelfrench.com

7 American Cinematheque

To listen to Hollywood actors and directors discuss movies, attend screenings by this group headquartered at the historic Egyptian Theatre (see p11 & p56). The schedule ranges from retrospectives to filmmaker tributes.

8 Margaret Herrick Library

It's easy to get lost in this vast repository of movie-related books and publications, operated by the Academy of Motion Picture Arts and Sciences. ⌾ Map L6 • 333 S La Cienega Blvd, Beverly Hills • 310-247-3000 • Open 10am–6pm Mon, Thu, & Fri, 10am–8pm Tue • Free (ID required)

9 It's a Wrap!

Much of the clothing worn by actors ends up here after the the final shot. There are bargains galore, and each item sports a tag identifying the show it appeared on. ⌾ Map D1 • 3315 W Magnolia Blvd, Burbank • 818-567-7366 • www.itsawraphollywood.com

10 Paramount Pictures Studio Tour

A 2-hour, behind-the-scenes tour. See the famous New York backlot and learn about the history of this working movie studio and Hollywood. Reservations required. ⌾ Map R4 • 5555 Melrose Ave • 323-956-1777 • Adm • www.paramountstudiotour.com

Top 10 LA Scandals

1 Fatty Arbuckle
Silent era funnyman was charged with the murder of actress Virginia Rappe in 1921, thus ending his career.

2 Errol Flynn
Hard-living swashbuckler whose penchant for teenage girls earned him a statutory rape charge in 1942.

3 Lana Turner
The actress's mobster lover was found stabbed to death in her house in 1958. Her teenage daughter, Cheryl Crane, took the blame.

4 Sharon Tate
Tate, 8 1/2 months pregnant, was among the victims of the Charles Manson murders in 1969.

5 John Belushi
A drug overdose ended this Blues Brother's life at age 33 in 1982 at the Chateau Marmont Hotel.

6 O.J. Simpson
The football star was cleared of the murder of his wife and her friend in 1994.

7 Heidi Fleiss
Infamous Hollywood madame, who ran an elite call-girl racket, received 37 months in jail in 1997.

8 George Michael
Pop singer was sentenced to a fine and community service in 1998 for lewd behavior in public.

9 Hugh Grant
Caught in a sexual act with a prostitute in his car, he was given two years' probation and a fine.

10 Winona Ryder
Actress convicted in 2002 of shoplifting $5,500 worth of goods; got probation, community service, and a fine.

Call up Celebrity Tours, in Palm Springs, at 888-805-2700 for a look at the lives of the area's most exclusive residents

Left **Conga Room** Right **El Rey Theatre**

Live Music Clubs

The Avalon Hollywood

El Rey Theatre
This hot live music venue was originally built in 1936 as an Art Deco theater with sweeping staircases, a VIP balcony lounge, and a grand ballroom. It's an all-ages, standing-room venue with a good, little café and an outside eating area. ⊗ *Map N6 • 5515 Wilshire Blvd • 323-936-6400 • Open for special events • www.theelrey.com*

Exchange LA
Located in the former Los Angeles Stock Exchange Building in the core of downtown Los Angeles, this opulent venue draws a dressed-up, hip crowd and features new acts and progressive, high-profile DJs. The completely renovated 1929 building spans four stories and more than 25,000 sq ft (2,323 sq m). ⊗ *Map V5 • 618 S Springs St • 213-627-8070 • Open 10am–2pm Fri–Sun • www.exchangela.com*

Conga Room
Backed by Jennifer Lopez, Jimmy Smits, and other celebrities, this club presents Latin and world music, with an emphasis on salsa, to a multi-cultural crowd *(see p100)*.

McCabe's Guitar Shop
The biggest names in folk music from Arlo Guthrie to Al Viola have played in the back room of this legendary acoustic instruments store. The no-frills, convivial setting appeals to true devotees. Moderate ticket prices and free coffee. ⊗ *Map C3 • 3101 Pico Blvd, Santa Monica • 310-828-4497 • Shows: usually Fri, Sat, & Sun • www.mccabes.com*

The Troubadour
Catch local and touring bands on their way to greatness – Elton John and Sheryl Crow have played here. The upstairs balcony offers good stage views, and there are three bars to keep the crowds lubricated. ⊗ *Map K4 • 9081 Santa Monica Blvd, West Hollywood • 310-276-6168 • Open daily*

McCabe's Guitar Shop façade

For movie theaters See pp56–7

6 The Avalon Hollywood

The old Hollywood Palace is now one of the hippest music and dance clubs. After live shows, DJs take over for house and techno dance music until the early hours. ⌾ Map Q2 • 1735 Vine St, Hollywood • 323-462-3000 • Open Fri & Sat & for special events • www.avalon hollywood.com

7 The Mayan

The Mayan is a salsa club that regularly books salsa, merengue, and Rock en Español bands. The dance menu includes funk, disco, house, and retro rhythms. Strict dress code. ⌾ Map S6 • 1038 S Hill St • 213-746-4287 • Open Fri & Sat & for special events • www.clubmayan.com

8 Harvelle's

One of LA's favorites for live blues, this is the oldest live music venue on the Westside. Both new artists and established musicians draw crowds, so get there early for a seat. ⌾ Map C3 • 1432 4th St Santa Monica • 310-395-1676 • Open daily • www.harvelles.com

9 Vibrato

World-class performances and sound design bring jazz aficionados flocking to this jazz and dinner club, owned by Herb Alpert. Dine on contemporary American cuisine or sip cocktails at the bar. ⌾ Map C2 • 2930 Beverly Glen Circle, Bel Air • 310-474-9400 • Open Tue–Sun • www.vibratogrilljazz.com

10 Upstairs at Vitello's

An intimate spot in a trendy neighborhood, this place consistently books top jazz artists. Acoustics are excellent and the restaurant downstairs serves better-than-average Italian dishes. ⌾ Map D2 • 4349 Tujunga Ave, Studio City • 818-769-0905 • Open Mon, Thu, & Sun & for special events • www.vitellosjazz.com

Top 10 Hotel Bars

1 W Bar
Sexy socialites and their beaus drape themselves around the sleek bar at the W Los Angeles (see p147).

2 Cameo Bar
Hollywood glamour goes seaside at this Neo-Colonial bar at the Viceroy (see p147).

3 The Mixing Room
Located in the JW Marriott at LA LIVE, this lounge specializes in innovative cocktails using house-made syrups. ⌾ Map S5 • 900 W Olympic Blvd • 213-765-8600

4 Rooftop Bar at the Standard Downtown
Ultra-cool spot with bird's-eye city views and unique water-beds for lounging (see p147).

5 Windows Lounge
Celebrity sightings are common at this swank bar at the Four Seasons (see p144).

6 The Tower Bar at Sunset Tower Hotel
Order martinis at this Sunset Strip haven with a decor reminiscent of Hollywood's Golden Era (see p146).

7 Oliverio
Hobnob with the fashion-able crowd while sipping a signature Blue Avalon (see p147).

8 Penthouse
A Thomas Schoos-designed lounge, bar, and restaurant in The Huntley Hotel. ⌾ Map A3 • 1111 2nd St, Santa Monica • 310-393-8080

9 Gallery Bar
A dark and quiet spot to unwind with cocktails in old-world grandeur at the stylish Millenium Biltmore (see p77).

10 Bar 1200 Cocktail Lab
The door policy might be tight, but you'll be mingling with celebs at the Sunset Marquis (see p65 & p147).

Left **Bunny Museum** Right **Million Dollar Pharmacy**

Weird & Wacky LA

1 Angelyne
American model, actress, and singer, Angelyne ostensibly became an icon of Los Angeles, principally because of the many billboards she purchased advertising herself. Styling herself as a real-life "Barbie," she drives a pink Chevrolet Corvette and keeps a pink Maltese dog. Her billboards have gained more fame than she has, featuring in several television shows and movies.

2 Necromance
If the sight of freeze-dried ducklings gives you the creeps, you should probably avoid this "little shop of horrors." Budding sorcerers and those in search of decorations for their own haunted mansions will find delightfully macabre stuff to buy. ✎ *Map P4*
• *7220 Melrose Ave • 323-934-8684*
• *www.necromance.com*

3 Dennis Woodruff
Dennis Woodruff is best known for being a non-celebrity. The "world's most famous

Necromance

unknown actor" can be seen around Hollywood in his outrageous vintage car decorated with lines such as "Buy my movie" or "Actor Awaiting his Break." Woodruff's elusive quest for fame was featured in Angelo Guglielmo's documentary *Idling Brando*.

4 Porno Walk of Fame
LA lays claim to the rather dubious title of "World Capital of the Adult Entertainment Industry." Its biggest legends of lust, including John Holmes and Linda Lovelace, have left their hand- and footprints in the sidewalk outside the former Pussycat movie theater. Renamed the Tomkat Theater, it now shows gay porn. ✎ *Map N3 • 7734 Santa Monica Blvd, Hollywood • 323-650-9551*

5 Skeletons in the Closet
Fancy a beach towel with a dead body outline? A coffee mug featuring a skeleton dressed up like Sherlock Holmes? A toe tag key chain? You'll find all these and more at this gift shop operated by the LA County Coroner and located right above the morgue. Proceeds benefit a county-run youth drunk driver alternative sentencing program. ✎ *Map E2*
• *1104 N Mission Rd, E of Downtown*
• *323-343-0760 • Open 8:30am–4:30pm Mon–Fri • www.lacoroner.com*

6 Million Dollar Pharmacy
The aisles of this bizarre "pharmacy" are packed with potions and powders said to cure

many ills, mostly of the aching heart variety. Wiping your floors with a vile liquid will banish evil spirits, while lighting a strange-smelling candle will bring you good fortune. They also have voodoo dolls, complete with an instruction leaflet, should you feel really wicked. § *Map V4 • 301 S Broadway, Downtown • 213-687-3688*

7 Farmer John Mural
It takes a morbid sense of humor to cover a sausage factory with a giant mural of verdant pastures with happy, frolicking pigs. But that's just what the Cloughertys, the family behind the Farmer John meat empire, did when they hired Les Grimes, a Hollywood set painter, in the late 1950s. Tourists have gone "hog-wild" ever since. § *Map E3 • 3049 E Vernon Ave, southwest of Downtown*

8 Bunny Museum
The private home of Candace Frazee and Steve Lubanski is a living museum filled with over 28,000 bunny collectibles. This is the world's largest bunny collection and includes old favorites such as Bugs Bunny, Peter Rabbit, Roger Rabbit, and Alice in Wonderland's March Hare. § *Map F1 • 1933 Jefferson Dr, Pasadena • 626-798-8848 • Open by appointment only • Free • www.thebunny museum.com*

9 Museum of Jurassic Technology
The doors of this bizarre museum open up a parallel universe where the seemingly mundane becomes extraordinary. Exhibits

Venice Boardwalk

include Cameroonian stink ants and American trailer park populations alongside an uncanny likeness of Pope John Paul II in the eye of a needle. Give in to this strange world and prepare to be mesmerized. § *Map C3 • 9341 Venice Blvd, Culver City • 310-836-6131 • Open 2–8pm Thu, noon–6pm Fri–Sun • Donation • www.mjt.org*

10 Venice Boardwalk
Venice's origins as an amusement park live on along the Venice Boardwalk. An endless parade of poseurs and eccentrics, from wiry street performers dancing on broken glass to steroid-enhanced musclemen, it remains a place where true freedom of expression reigns *(see p122)*.

Left **Viper Room** Right **Spago Beverly Hills**

🔟 Places to See & Be Seen

Fred Segal
Today's hottest stars such as Jennifer Aniston, Nicole Kidman, and George Clooney have all been spotted browsing for cool clothes and accessories at this style emporium. It's also a favorite for wardrobe buyers for TV and feature films. The West Hollywood branch is more celebrity-heavy *(see p108)*.

Urth Caffè
This West Hollywood eating joint is a health- and waist-conscious café on the celebrity radar, but most days it's just the usual in-crowd munching on vegetarian lasagne and noshing on New York cheesecake. The sunny patio offers the best vantage point for checking out the crowd from behind sunglasses. 🅢 *Map L4 • 8565 Melrose Ave, West Hollywood • 310-659-0628*

Viper Room
Celebrities like to hang out with their own kind and this place got its start with Johnny Depp, one of the original owners. It still has enormous cachet, with standing room only for the crowds who come to see and be seen. It's best known as a place to see the freshest, hippest new bands *(see p9 & p106)*.

The Ivy
The air at this rustic French restaurant is electric with the buzz of Hollywood's power players. Deals are struck daily between movie moguls, celebs, agents, and their high-profile clients. Count yourself fortunate if you manage to score a table on the fenced-in patio table for great people and celeb watching. 🅢 *Map L5 • 113 N Robertson Blvd, West Hollywood • 310-274-8303*

Fred Segal

Spago Beverly Hills

There aren't too many restaurants whose owners are as famous as their A-list patrons, but Wolfgang Puck is certainly one of them. He can often be seen schmoozing in the dining room and blowing air kisses. One of the most pleasant spots for stargazing (see p67 & p115).

Book Soup

This excellent independent bookstore draws a sizeable celebrity contingent with its eclectic offerings, including international publications. Try and increase your chances of meeting a star by attending one of their book readings or book signing sessions. Call for schedules. ✆ Map L3 • 8818 Sunset Blvd, West Hollywood • 310-659-3110, 1-800-764-BOOK (toll free)

Bar 1200 Cocktail Lab

Catering to a "Rolls-Royce" rock'n'roll crowd, this hot hangout at the Sunset Marquis Hotel (see p61 & p147) was once owned by Rande Gerber, husband of supermodel Cindy Crawford. Getting past the velvet rope isn't easy, especially when big names such as Bono from U2 come by.

Barneys New York

Max out your credit card while keeping an eye out for superstars and celebrities at this luxurious department store. All the major designers from Armani to Helmut Lang and Dolce & Gabbana are represented here. Take in the nice views from the outdoor tables in the rooftop deli. ✆ Map J6 • 9570 Wilshire Blvd, Beverly Hills • 310-276-4400

The Staples Center

LA Lakers Games at Staples Center

The Los Angeles Lakers, the city's fabled basketball team, always attract a fair number of celebrities to their games at the Staples Center (see p46). Number One fan, Jack Nicholson, can usually be spotted courtside, and Denzel Washington and Eddie Murphy are regulars. Leonardo DiCaprio, Jennifer Lopez, and Ben Affleck have also made appearances.

Chateau Marmont & Bar Marmont

Celebrities have flocked to this European-style hotel like moths to the flame since its opening way back in 1929. Famed for its discretion, it has remained a favorite spot for celebrity trysts. Check out the chic Bar Marmont (see p8, p106, & p146).

Left **Lobster on display in Water Grill** Right **Valentino**

TOP 10 Restaurants

The Patina sign

1 Patina
A long-time darling of food critics and gourmets, Patina is where star chef Joachim Splichal takes his innovative French-California cuisine to new heights. The melt-in-your-mouth *côte de boeuf*, served table-side, is indicative of the kitchen's lofty aspirations. Try the chef's superb tasting menu. ⊗ Map U4 • Walt Disney Concert Hall, 141 S Grand Ave • 213-972-3331 • $$$$

2 Water Grill
A premier seafood joint, this is usually packed to the gills with patrons appreciative of the dock-fresh fare and superb service. Chef Michael Cimarusti turns each dish into a culinary celebration of bold flavors and pleasing textures. The yummy white clam chouder and hand-cut tuna tartare are outstanding, and the oyster bar scores high with the pre-theater crowd *(see p79)*.

3 Providence
Don't be fooled by this restaurant's bland exterior. It is an LA institution serving some of the West Coast's best seafood. From the series of separate, elegant dining areas, choose the intimate patio room if you are in search of a romantic evening.

Fresh truffles are a specialty, as are the changing tasting menus and wine pairings.

4 Echigo
Excellent, imaginatively presented sushi of all types is the only offering at this eatery. The ambience is simple and plain, with only 12 seats at the L-shaped bar. Service is attentive. Angelenos have been raving about this place since it opened around 10 years ago. The *omakase* (chef's choice) is outstanding *(see p109)*.

5 Matsuhisa
This is the original of a small chain of restaurants serving Nobu Matsuhisa's inspired Japanese-Peruvian fusion fare. The sushi is impeccable and the tempura extra-light, but the chef's talent really lies in cooked seafood dishes, many paired with Nobu's perky sauces. Celebrity sightings

Spago Beverly Hills

For more restaurants and a key to price categories See pp79, 85, 93, 101, 109, 115, 125, 131 are likely. Make reservations several days in advance to avoid the rush (see p115).

Spago Beverly Hills
This beautiful Wolfgang Puck outpost is a favorite with the rich and famous and a great place to sample California cuisine. The chef keeps the menu in flux but always pairs supreme cuts of meat or fish with seasonal side dishes such as chanterelle mushrooms. The lox pizza is always popular. Early reservations essential (see p65 & p115).

Michael's
A pioneer of California cuisine, Michael's serves Oscarworthy cuisine in a luscious garden setting, making it one of the best alfresco dining spots in all LA. The food delights eye and palate. ⊗ Map A3 • 1147 3rd St, Santa Monica • 310-451-0843 • Dis. access • Accepts credit cards • Veg: Yes • $$$

Mélisse
Consistently ranked as the top food in LA, Josiah Citrin's Mélisse uses fresh local ingredients to create classic French cuisine with a modern twist. Seasonal white truffle and game menus also feature. A gorgeous dining room and expertly trained staff add to a dining experience that borders on perfection. ⊗ Map B3 • 1104 Wilshire Blvd, Santa Monica • 310-395-0881 • Dis. access • Accepts credit cards • Veg: Yes • $$$$$

Joe's Main Street Diner
Joe Miller is one of LA's most dedicated and competent chefs, and his excellent French-infused California cuisine has

Entrance to Joe's Main Street Diner

leagues of loyal fans. Using only fresh, seasonal ingredients, Miller shows off his talent with frequently changing menus. The *prix fixe* dinners are good value, while lunches are a real steal. Dinner reservations are a must to avoid disappointment later (see p125).

Valentino
For over 30 years, Piero Selvaggio has delighted diners with his charm and inspired Italian cuisine. His 150,000 plus cellar of handpicked wines from all regions of the Boot is outstanding. So are the ingredients, many of them imported from the old country. Insiders ignore the menu and try the "extravaganza," a series of delicious treats.
⊗ Map C3 • 3115 Pico Blvd, Santa Monica • 310-829-4313 • Dis. access • Accepts credit cards • Veg: Yes • $

AROUND TOWN

LOS ANGELES TOP 10

4C
er
um
1/4 MI

NAVAL AND
MARINE CORPS
RESERVE CENTER
NEXT EXIT

Left **Olvera Street marketplace, El Pueblo de Los Angeles** Right **Union Station**

Downtown

DOWNTOWN LA IS A MICROCOSM *of the city's past, present, and future and one of its most intriguing neighborhoods. El Pueblo commemorates the city's Spanish origins, while Chinatown to the north and Little Tokyo to the south are the vibrant centers of immigrant communities. The city's financial pulse beats in glass high-rises along Flower and Figueroa Streets in sharp contrast to the eclectic early 20th-century architecture in the area around Pershing Square. Culture is king in Downtown, from the renowned Museum of Contemporary Art and the spectacular Walt Disney Concert Hall to the experimental galleries and studios of the Arts District east of Alameda Avenue. The Fashion and Jewelry Districts also add their own flair to the urban tapestry, and Downtown is dominated by L.A. Live, a vast sports and entertainment district. The area is eminently walkable, but DASH buses also run between the diverse worlds that make up LA.*

Restaurant in Chinatown

🔟 Downtown Sights

1. El Pueblo de Los Angeles
2. Union Station
3. Chinatown
4. Little Tokyo
5. City Hall
6. Cathedral of Our Lady of the Angels
7. Walt Disney Concert Hall
8. Museum of Contemporary Art (MOCA)
9. L.A. Live Sports and Entertainment District
10. Grand Central Market

Union Station

El Pueblo de Los Angeles

This historic district near LA's 1781 founding site comprises buildings dating back to the early 19th century, when the city was little more than a scruffy outpost under Mexican rule. Its main artery, Olvera Street, has been restored to a lively lane lined with Mexican trinket shops and restaurants *(see pp20–21)*.

Union Station

Built in 1939 during the golden age of railroad travel, the design of the dignified Union Station blends traditional Spanish Mission elements with Modernist Art Deco touches. Its lofty main waiting room is graced with a coffered wooden ceiling, highly polished marble floors, and tall arched windows. Union Station has been featured in several movies, *The Hustler* (1961) and *Bugsy* (1992) among others. ⓢ *Map X4 • 800 N Alameda St*

Chinatown

The Chinese first settled in LA after the Gold Rush, but were forced by the construction of Union Station to relocate a few blocks north to an area that is today known as "New Chinatown." The cultural hub of over 200,000 Chinese Americans, this exotic district has stores hawking dried and pickled ginger and lucky bamboo, the offices of herbalists and acupuncturists, and restaurants that serve hot dim sum. In February, the Chinese New Year is celebrated with colorful parades and dragon dances. ⓢ *Map W2 • Along Broadway Hill north of Cesar Chavez Blvd*

Little Tokyo

The Japanese have been a presence in LA since the 1880s, but radical redevelopment in the 1960s replaced most of Little Tokyo's original structures with bland modern architecture. The few surviving buildings on East First Street are now protected as a National Historic Landmark. Stop at the Japanese American National Museum *(see p76)*, and check out the MOCA Geffen Contemporary *(see p76)* close by, and the Japanese Village Plaza. ⓢ *Map W5 • Bounded by 1st & 4th, Alameda, & Los Angeles Sts*

Japanese American National Museum

Chung King Road Galleries

This quiet, lantern-festooned lane in western Chinatown is the hotbed of LA's art scene. Artists' studios and no fewer than eight galleries have opened in between the traditional Chinese antique and furniture stores in the area. Follow a browsing session with a quiet drink at the venerable Hop Louie restaurant.

5 City Hall

LA's tallest building for over four decades, the central tower of this 1928 shiny white Downtown presence was three times higher than the then height limit. Renovations have made it possible for the public to admire its marble-columned rotunda once again. City Hall has been immortalized on celluloid countless times, most famously as the headquarters of the *Daily Planet* in the *Superman* TV series. It was also attacked by Martians in *The War of the Worlds* (1954). ◈ *Map W4 • 200 N Spring St • Open 8am–5pm Mon–Fri • Guided tours: 10am–noon • Free*

6 Cathedral of Our Lady of the Angels

LA's strikingly modern Roman Catholic cathedral looms above the Hollywood Freeway that has been likened to a "river of transportation." The adobe-colored structure is entered through giant bronze doors cast by LA sculptor Robert Graham and guarded by a statue of Our Lady of the Angels. The soaring hall of worship, which can seat up to 3,000 people, is bathed in soft light streaming in through the alabaster windows. It is the first Catholic cathedral to be constructed in the western US in over a quarter century. ◈ *Map V3 • 555 W Temple St • 213-680-5200 • Open 6:30am–6pm Mon–Fri, 9am–6pm Sat, 7am–6pm Sun • Free tours: 1pm Mon–Fri • www.olacathedral.org*

7 Walt Disney Concert Hall

The home of the Los Angeles Philharmonic Orchestra (directed by Esa Pekka Salonen since 1991) is a spectacular addition to Downtown's physical and cultural landscape. Frank Gehry conceived the dramatic design of this 2,265-seat auditorium, rather like the sculptural interpretation of a ship caught at sea. The exterior "sails" are clad in shining stainless steel panels, while the concert space itself boasts a curved wooden ceiling carefully calibrated for superb acoustics. ◈ *Map V4 • 111 S Grand Ave • 323-850-2000 • www.laphil.com*

8 Museum of Contemporary Art (MOCA)

An early player in Downtown's cultural renaissance, MOCA collects and displays art in all media from 1940 to the present. Works by Jackson Pollock, Andy Warhol, and Roy Lichtenstein form part of its permanent collection. The museum building, designed by famous Japanese architect Arata Isozaki, is a jumble of cubes, pyramids, and other shapes in reddish stone. ◈ *Map U4 • 250 S Grand Ave • 213-626-6222 • Open 11am–5pm Mon & Fri, 11am–8pm Thu, 11am–6pm Sat & Sun • Adm (free after 5pm on Thu) • www.moca.org*

Rotunda in City Hall

Note: MOCA tickets are good for same-day entry at MOCA Geffen Contemporary and within 30 days at MOCA (Pacific Design Center)

Grand Central Market

9 L.A. Live Sports and Entertainment District

A 4,000,000 sq ft (371,600 sq m) development, adjoining the Staples Center and the Los Angeles Convention Center, created LA's premier sports and entertainment district. It contains an exciting mix of entertainment venues, restaurants, retail outlets, luxury hotels, and private residences. Venues include the NOKIA Theatre, with state-of-the-art acoustics and seating for 7,200 people, and Club NOKIA, a live music venue. At the heart of the center is the open-air NOKIA Plaza. ⊗ *Map S6*

10 Grand Central Market

Angelenos have perused the produce aisles of this exotic and lively market since 1917. Today, visitors stock up on everything from fruits and vegetables to fresh fish and meat, and spices and herbs to cakes and bread, all available at bargain prices. Many of the eateries here also have long traditions, such as Roast-to-Go where the Penilla family has served made-to-order tacos and burritos since the 1950s. The architect Frank Lloyd Wright once had an office upstairs in this 1905 Beaux-Arts building. ⊗ *Map V5 • 317 S Broadway • 213-624-2378 • Open 9am–6pm daily • www.grand centralsquare.com*

A Day in Downtown

Morning

🕐 Begin your day with the historic **El Pueblo**, which will take you back to the city's vibrant Mexican and Spanish past. Browse colorful **Olvera Street** for authentic crafts and food, and then cross Alameda Street for a close-up of the grand **Union Station**.

Next, go west along Cesar E Chavez Avenue, before turning right on Broadway for a stroll through exotic **Chinatown** and a superb dim sum lunch at the **Empress Pavilion** *(see p79)*.

Afternoon

Ride the DASH bus "B" from Broadway to Temple Street, dominated by the **Cathedral of Our Lady of the Angels**. After admiring Rafael Moneo's Modernist masterpiece, head south along Grand Avenue, past the **Music Center** *(see p54)* and the **Walt Disney Concert Hall** *(see p54)* to check out the latest exhibits at the **MOCA**.

Stroll down **Bunker Hill Steps** *(see p77)*, stopping to gaze at "Source Figure," Robert Graham's exquisite sculpture and the **Central Library** *(see p76)*. Walk to **Pershing Square** *(see p76)*, lorded over by the baronial **Millennium Biltmore Hotel** *(see p77)*, a nice place for tea or coffee. Leave in time to make it to the Victorian **Bradbury Building** before 5pm. Browse for treasures in the bountiful aisles of the **Grand Central Market**.

To get back to El Pueblo, board DASH bus "D" on Spring Street, changing to "B" at Temple Street.

Left **Central Library** Right **Pershing Square**

TOP 10 Best of the Rest

1 Wells Fargo History Museum

This little museum relives the days of the Wild West and houses an original stagecoach and a gold nugget from the Gold Rush.
◈ Map U4 • 333 S Grand Ave • Open 9am–5pm Mon–Fri • Free

2 Central Library

LA's main library consists of the original 1926 building, an exotic Beaux-Arts design by Bertram Goodhue, and an art-filled atrium added in 1993.
◈ Map U5 • 630 W 5th St • 213-228-7000 • Open 10am–8pm Mon–Thu, 10am–5:30pm Fri–Sat

3 Pershing Square

The city's oldest public park, redesigned in the early 1990s, it is enlivened with public art and flanked by numerous historic buildings, most notably the grand Biltmore. Wi-Fi available. ◈ Map U5

4 Jewelry District

Precious gems, watches, and all kinds of fine jewelry are sold in shops in what has long been the center of Los Angeles's jewelry industry. ◈ Map U5 • Hill St just off Pershing Square

5 Fashion District

This 56-block district is the heart of LA's clothing industry (the largest in the nation) and heaven on earth for bargain hunters (see p53). ◈ Map U6
• Bounded by Broadway, San Pedro St, 7th St, & 16th St

6 Flower Market

This 1913 cut-flower market, the largest in the country, has it all from roses to orchids. ◈ Map V6 • 766 Wall St • 213-627-3696 • Open 8am–noon Mon & Wed, 6am–11am Tue & Thu, 8am–2pm Fri, 6am–2pm Sat • Adm
• www.originallaflowermarket.com

7 Toy District

A 14-block area selling a wide range of traditional toys, electronics, silk flowers, and other odds and ends, this is a lively spot, especially on week-ends. ◈ Map V5 • Bounded by 3rd and 5th Sts, Werdin Place, & San Pedro St

8 Japanese American National Museum

Housed in a Buddhist temple, this museum chronicles the history of Japanese Americans.
◈ Map W5 • 100 N Central Ave • 213-625-0414 • Open 11am–5pm Tue, Wed, Fri–Sun, noon–8pm Thu • Adm • www.janm.org

9 MOCA Geffen Contemporary

This huge former police garage hosts traveling shows and special exhibits. ◈ Map W5 • 152 N Central Ave • 213-626-6222 • Open 11am–5pm Mon & Fri, 11am–8pm Thu, 11am–6pm Sat & Sun • Adm • www.moca.org

10 Downtown Arts District

As artists move into studios here, hip galleries, shops, and restaurants have opened. ◈ Map U4 • Bounded by 1st & 7th Sts, Alameda Ave, & the Los Angeles River

The Whole Foods Market at 239 North Crescent Drive has an enormous array of health food

Left **Westin Bonaventure** Center **Millennium Biltmore** Right **Eastern Columbia Building**

 # Downtown Architecture

1 Oviatt Building
This 1927 Art Deco gem features French fixtures and a forecourt adorned with Lalique glass. It houses the popular Cicada restaurant (see p79).
◈ Map U5 • 617 S Olive St

2 US Bank Tower
Shooting upward for about 1,017 ft (305 m), this building was erected only after developers were forced to purchase the air rights from neighboring Central Library in order to exceed official height limits.
◈ Map U5 • 633 W 5th St

3 Westin Bonaventure Hotel
The five mirror-glass cylinders of LA's biggest hotel look like a giant space ship ready for take-off (see p150). ◈ Map U4
• 404 S Figueroa St • 213-624-1000

4 Old Bank District
This trio of statuesque buildings, built between 1904 and 1910, has been converted into upscale residential lofts.
◈ Map V5 • On 4th St between Main & Spring Sts

5 Millennium Biltmore Hotel
This palatial 1923 Beaux-Arts extravaganza includes architectural styles ranging from Renaissance to Neo-Classical.
◈ Map U5 • 506 S Grand Ave • 213-624-1011

6 Fine Arts Building
Behind the richly detailed façade of this 1927 building awaits an amazing galleried lobby in Spanish Renaissance style.
◈ Map T5 • 811 W 7th St Lobby
• Open during office hours

7 Bunker Hill Steps
Cascading down from Hope Street to Fifth Street, these steps have many attractive features, including an amazing sculpture of a female nude by Robert Graham (see p78). ◈ Map U4

8 Eastern Columbia Building
This former 1930s furniture and clothing store has a bright turquoise terracotta mantle and now houses loft apartments.
◈ Map U6 • 849 Broadway

9 Coca-Cola Bottling Plant
This Streamline Moderne building, located in an industrial area, resembles an ocean liner, complete with porthole windows. Two giant Coke bottles guard the corners. ◈ Map E3 • 1334 S Central Ave • Not open to the public

10 Broadway Historic Theater District
During the silent film era, Broadway was the movie district. The façades of the movie palaces are marvels of the imagination.
◈ Map U6 • Along Broadway between 3rd & 9th Sts

Left *Peace on Earth* by Jacques Lipchitz Center & Right *Traveler* by Terry Schoonhoven

TOP 10 Public Art

1 Peace on Earth
Created at the height of the Vietnam War in 1969, Jacques Lipchitz's large bronze Madonna has the dove, a symbol of peace, on top, and lambs, representing humanity, at the base. ✎ *Map V4 • Music Center Plaza, 135 N Grand Ave*

2 Four Arches
Alexander Calder is best known for his mobiles, but this looming 1975 steel work painted in glowing fiery orange-red is a "stabile," an abstract stationary sculpture. ✎ *Map U4 • 333 S Hope St*

3 Wells Fargo Court
The ground floor of this office complex is a treasure trove of public art with nudes by Robert Graham, Joan Miró's childlike *La Caresse d'un Oiseau*, and Jean Dubuffet's cartoonish *Le Dandy*. ✎ *Map U4 • Wells Fargo Center, 333 S Grand Ave*

4 Source Figure
This bronze African-American female nude overlooks the Bunker Hill Steps *(see p77)*. Designed by Robert Graham in 1992, she represents the source of the water cascading down the stairs. ✎ *Map U4 • Hope St, near 4th St*

5 Corporate Head
This evocative sculpture (1990) by Terry Allen and Philip Levine condemns the greed and erosion of moral responsibility in today's corporate America. ✎ *Map T5 • 725 S Figueroa St*

6 Spine
This 1993 installation by Jud Fine is a visual allegory of a book – the well symbolizes the title page, the step risers the pages, and the pools the plot flow. ✎ *Map U4 • Maguire Gardens, northern side of Central Library, Flower, & 5th Sts*

7 Biddy Mason: A Passage of Time
This memorial by Betye Saar and Sheila de Bretteville commemorates the story of former slave, Biddy Mason (1818–91), a leader who established the city's first black church. ✎ *Map V5 • 333 S Spring St, near 3rd St*

8 Astronaut Ellison S. Onizuka Memorial
A 1/10th scale model of the *Challenger*, this 1990 memorial by Isao Hirai honors the first Japanese-American astronaut. ✎ *Map W5 • Onizuka St, Little Tokyo*

9 Molecule Man
This monumental 1991 sculpture by Jonathan Borofsky shows four embracing figures, symbolizing the commonality between people based on their shared molecular structure. ✎ *Map W4 • 255 E Temple St*

10 Traveler
Terry Schoonhoven's 1993 ceramic mural depicts California travelers from the days of the Spanish explorations, and LA landmarks such as Pico House *(see p21)*. ✎ *Map X4 • Union Station*

Price Categories

Price categories include a three-course meal for one, a glass of house wine, and all unavoidable extra charges including tax.

$	under $25
$$	$25–$50
$$$	$50–$80
$$$$	over $80

Cole's

Places to Eat

1 Water Grill
Fish and seafood fanciers from all over flock to this clubby shrine, which uses only impeccably fresh ingredients. Desserts are superb. ✆ *Map U5 • 544 S Grand Ave • 213-891-0900 • $$$*

2 Cicada
The sumptuous Art Deco dining room in the historic Oviatt Building almost overshadows the food. The Northern Italian menu features classics. ✆ *Map U5 • 617 S Olive St • 213-488-9488 • $$$*

3 Engine Co. No. 28
This former firehouse serves American comfort food with top ingredients. A favorite for business lunches, theater-goers, and Lakers fans. ✆ *Map U5 • 644 Figueroa St • 213-624-6996 • $$$$*

4 Nick & Stef's Steakhouse
Loosen your belt for the juiciest steaks ever. Preview your cut in the glass-encased aging chamber. ✆ *Map U4 • 330 S Hope St, Wells Fargo Center • 213-680-0330 • $$$*

5 McCormick & Schmick's
This vast wood and leather seafood restaurant has the city's finest Happy Hours with fish tacos, stir-fried rice, and other fun fare at bargain prices. ✆ *Map U4 • 633 W 5th St • 213-629-1929 • $$*

6 Cole's
This dimly lit eatery serves beef, pork, lamb, and turkey sandwiches. Side dishes and seasonal pies round off the menu. No veggie options. ✆ *Map U5 • 118 E 6th St • 213-622-4090 • $*

7 Empress Pavilion
For great dim sum, snag a table in this Chinatown banquet hall. Try the bite-sized stuffed wontons and short ribs. ✆ *Map W2 • 988 N Hill St, Bamboo Plaza • 213-617-9898 • $*

8 Yang Chow
In this reliable Chinese eatery, a plate of the hallmark "slippery shrimp" graces almost every table. The *moo-shu* pork is also a good bet. ✆ *Map W2 • 819 N Broadway, Chinatown • 213-625-0811 • $*

9 R-23
Canvases adorn the walls of this sophisticated sushi parlor in a former warehouse in the Arts District. The raw fish morsels are divine. ✆ *Map X5 • 923 E 2nd St • 213-687-7178 • Closed Sun • $$$*

10 Casa La Dona
A salsa bar with truly authentic regional dishes from Mexico, home-made tortillas, great tamales, and spot-on service. Try the fresh blue-gill fish. ✆ *Map U6 • 800 S Main St • 213-627-7441 • Open daily, breakfast only Fri–Sun • $*

Unless otherwise stated, all restaurants accept credit cards, serve vegetarian meals, and provide access for the disabled

Left **Dodger Stadium** Center **California African American Museum** Right **Southwest Museum**

Around Downtown

I T HAS BEEN SAID THAT LA IS NOT *really a city, but a collection of 88 independent towns that overlap. Nowhere is this truer than within the 5-mile (8-km) radius of the center of Downtown. West of here, Koreatown is home to the largest Korean population in the US, while east LA has the largest group of Latinos living outside Latin America. In the Latino-Byzantine quarter, surrounding the Greek Orthodox St. Sophia Cathedral on Normandie Avenue, Latinos and Greeks pre-*

dominate and complement each other. Northeast of Downtown is Dodger Stadium, a world-famous landmark, while south of the center lies Exposition Park with its museums and sports venues. This area constitutes a melting pot for people belonging to different races and geographical regions. America needs no better mirror than the city of Los Angeles to see what it will one day surely become.

Natural History Museum

🔟 Sights

1. Natural History Museum
2. California African American Museum
3. California Science Center
4. Dodger Stadium
5. Angelino Heights
6. Heritage Square Museum
7. Charles F. Lummis Home and Garden
8. Southwest Museum of the American Indian
9. St. Sophia Cathedral
10. San Antonio Winery

1 Natural History Museum

It's easy to spend a day exploring this engaging museum, the nation's second largest of its kind. The dinosaurs always draw huge crowds, as does the Age of Mammals exhibit with the Simi Valley mastodon, and the grisly 14.5-ft (4-m) long megamouth, the rarest shark in the world. The Gem and Mineral Hall contains a huge gold exhibit and a dazzling walk-through gem vault. Cultural exhibits explain and highlight the traditions of Native and Latin American civilizations. Children love the hands-on activities in the Discovery Center and the Insect Zoo. ⊗ *Map D3 • 900 Exposition Blvd, Exposition Park • 213-763-3466 • Open 9:30am–5pm daily • Adm (free for under 5s) • www.nhm.org*

2 California African American Museum

This museum celebrates the art, history, and culture of African Americans, especially in relation to California and the western US. The main exhibit traces the journey from Africa to slavery in the American South to final freedom on the West Coast. It includes memorabilia donated by singer Ella Fitzgerald and former LA mayor Tom Bradley. Temporary shows highlight particular artists, including emerging ones. ⊗ *Map D3 • 600 State Dr, Exposition Park • 213-744-7432 • Open 10am–5pm Tue–Sat, 11am–5pm Sun • Free (parking $10) • www.caamuseum.org*

3 California Science Center

Filled with clever and engaging interactive exhibits, this highly entertaining science and technology museum has three themed galleries. The World of Life exhibit explains the processes living organisms undergo, Creative World focuses on the ability of humans to adapt to their environment through technology, and the Air and Space Gallery explores the great beyond. But it's a 50-ft (15-m) long animatronic doll stripped down to her organs that steals the show and attracts crowds. ⊗ *Map D3 • 700 State Drive, Exposition Park • 323-724-3623 • Open 10am–5pm daily • Free (parking $10) • www.californiasciencecenter.org*

4 Dodger Stadium

For many, spring wouldn't be the same without baseball. The pilgrimage to Dodger Stadium to watch the "Boys in Blue" fight it out is an annual ritual for thousands of fans. Hunkered in the bleachers, munching on the famous Dodger Dogs, they watch their team (LA Dodgers) in action. The stadium opened in 1962 and is often called one of USA's most beautiful ballparks. It has hosted eight World Series, many concerts, and even a papal mass. ⊗ *Map W1 • 1000 Elysian Park Ave • 323-224-1448 • Tours (on non-game days by appointment only), tickets required • http://dodgers.mlb.com/la/ballpark*

California Science Center

Koreatown

Parts of western Vermont Avenue around Wilshire Boulevard west of Downtown would not look out of place in Seoul. They are the main arteries of Koreatown, which is home to the largest Korean population in the US and a beehive of commercial activity. Learn more about the Korean community at the Korean Cultural Center at 5505 Wilshire Blvd.

Angelino Heights

In the 1880s, this was one of LA's first suburbs and an elegant neighborhood with stately Victorian mansions along streets such as Carroll Avenue and Kellam Avenue. Many surviving buildings have been lovingly restored by their current owners. The 1300 block of Carroll Avenue has the finest, including the Haskin House at No. 1344 and the Foy House at No. 1325. They are open to the public only during tours run by the LA Conservancy (see p138). ⊗ Map U1 • Carroll Ave & Kellam Ave, Echo Park

Heritage Square Museum

Unlike those on Carroll Avenue, most other Victorian homes were demolished. A few, however, were moved by helicopter to form the Heritage Square Museum. Eight vintage beauties cluster here – five residences, a church, a barn, and a railroad depot that is also a visitor center, all sporting gables and turrets. The Hale House, impressively restored, stands out from the rest. ⊗ Map E2 • 3800 Homer St, Highland Park • 323-225-2700 • Open noon–5pm Fri–Sun (Oct–Mar: hours may vary, call for details) • Adm • www. heritagesquare.org

Hale House, Heritage Square Museum

Charles F. Lummis Home and Garden

Now the headquarters of the Historical Society of Southern California, this was once the home of the eccentric Charles Fletcher Lummis (1859–1928), who walked the entire 3,000 miles (4,830 km) from Ohio to LA in 1885. An outspoken California booster and preservationist, Lummis built his house with his own hands out of concrete and found materials, including boulders and railroad rails. The house is also known as El Alisal, the Spanish word for "sycamore," due to the giant sycamore by the building. ⊗ Map E2 • 200 E Ave 43, Highland Park • 323-222-0546 • Open noon–4pm Fri–Sun • Donation

Charles F. Lummis Home and Garden

Southwest Museum of the American Indian

The oldest museum in Los Angeles was the brainchild of Charles Lummis, whose personal collection of Native American artifacts formed the basis of its holdings. It has one of the nation's largest and most important collections of Native art and artifacts. Galleries provide a survey of the traditions of Native cultures from California, the Great Plains, the Southwest, and the Pacific Northwest. A famous collection of baskets is an intriguing exhibit. Restoration work is ongoing; call ahead for details. ✆ Map E2 • 234 Museum Dr, Highland Park • 323-221-2164 • Open 10am–4pm Sat (call for details) • Free • www.theautry.org

A Sequoyah Indian relief, Southwest Museum

St. Sophia Cathedral
One of LA's surprises, this central church of Southern California's Greek community was masterminded by the Skouras brothers, a trio of movie impresarios. Behind its austere exterior is an opulent hall of worship. The eye is drawn to the icon-studded, golden altar of the Virgin Mary while Jesus, surrounded by saints, looks down at the congregation from the 90-ft (27-m) high dome. ✆ Map D3 • 1324 S Normandie Ave, Koreatown • 323-737-2424 • Open 10am–4pm Tue–Fri, 10am–2pm Sat, 12:30–2pm Sun • Free • www.stsophia.org

San Antonio Winery
LA's only surviving winery is tucked away in the industrial area north of the Los Angeles River. It's hard to imagine that this bleak area was once blanketed with vineyards. When the founder of San Antonio, Santo Cambianica, arrived in 1917, he faced stiff competition from over 100 wineries. Prohibition put most out of business, but Santo survived making sacramental wine. Even today, fermentation continues to take place here. Taste the wines; the restaurant is a popular lunch spot (see p85). ✆ Map E2 • 737 Lamar St, Lincoln Heights, 323-223-1401, www.sanantonio winery.com • Tasting room open 9am–7pm Sun–Thu, 9am–8pm Fri & Sat • Free

Exploring Exposition Park in a Day

Morning

Start at **Exposition Park** from Figueroa Street and make the **Natural History Museum** the first stop of the day. Admire its lovely façade, before delving into the exhibits inside. A landmark bronze sculpture of a *Tyrannosaurus rex* battling a Triceratops stands to the north outside. Crossing the street takes you to the **University of Southern California** campus (see p84), where you can join a free guided tour offered hourly from 10am to 3pm. Have lunch on campus or walk east on Exposition Boulevard to the **Mercado La Paloma,** a Latin-flavored community center with colorful crafts stalls and casual eating joints.

Afternoon

Backtrack to Exposition Park and start the afternoon with a look at the **Los Angeles Memorial Coliseum** (see p47), the main venue of the 1932 and 1984 Olympics. The two huge headless bronze figures outside the eastern entrance were designed by local sculptor Robert Graham. Just north of here is the **California Science Center,** with many interactive exhibits. Grab a cold drink from the downstairs cafeteria and head outside to the fragrant **Rose Garden** (see p42) to relax. If you still have the energy left, do check out the store at the **California African American Museum**. Otherwise, wind down the day with a 3D visual adventure at the **IMAX Theater** (see p57) next to the Science Center.

Left **Shrine Auditorium** Right **Boots at El Mercado**

🔟 Best of the Rest

1 Angelus Temple
Founded by a popular preacher with a flair for theatrics, this 1923 domed building was once the headquarters of the Foursquare Gospel Church.
◈ Map E1 • 1100 Glendale Blvd, Echo Park • Open only during special events

2 The Wiltern
This live concert venue is encased by the lovely 1931 Art Deco Pelissier Building. ◈ Map D2 • 3790 Wilshire Blvd, Koreatown

3 Bullocks Wilshire Building
One of the earliest Art Deco structures in the country, this beautiful building now houses the Southwestern University School of Law. ◈ Map D2 • 3050 Wilshire Blvd, Koreatown

4 Shrine Auditorium
This 1926 Moorish-style theater seats up to 6,700 and was once the largest in the United States. ◈ Map D3 • 665 W Jefferson Blvd, Exposition Park area

5 University of Southern California (USC)
Built in 1880, the oldest private university in Western US counts George Lucas in its alumni. ◈ Map D3 • Bounded by Jefferson, Figueroa, Exposition Blvds, & Vermont Ave, Exposition Park area • 213-740-2311 • www.usc.edu

6 William Andrews Clark Memorial Library
This 1926 building has a rare collection of English books only available to scholars, and an oak-paneled music room. ◈ Map D3 • 2520 Cimarron St, W Adams district • 323-735-7605 • Tours by appointment

7 El Mercado
This indoor marketplace offers a peek into Mexican-American culture. Stop for an authentic meal or browse colorful stalls. ◈ Map E3 • 3425 E 1st St, E LA • 323-268-3451 • Open 10am–8pm Mon–Fri, 9am–9pm Sat & Sun

8 Self-help Graphics & Arts
This nonprofit arts center works chiefly with the Latino community. Visit the Galerias Otra Vez. ◈ Map E3 • 3802 Cesar E Chavez Ave, E LA • 323-881-6444 • Gallery hours: 10am–4pm Tue–Sat • Free

9 Mariachi Plaza
Mariachi musicians in black robes gather in this small park, waiting to be hired for the night's engagements. ◈ Map E2 • Corner of Boyle Ave & 1st St, E LA

10 Brewery Arts Complex
This massive artist colony organizes art walks twice yearly.
◈ Map E2 • 2100 N Main St, Lincoln Heights • 323-441-9593 • Gallery open Fri–Sun (by appointment) • Free

Price Categories

Price categories include a three-course meal for one, a glass of house wine, and all unavoidable extra charges including tax.

$	under $25
$$	$25–$50
$$$	$50–$80
$$$$	over $80

Guelaguetza

🔟 Places to Eat

1 Maddalena Restaurant
This slice of Italy, in what was once the fermentation cellars of the San Antonio Winery (see p83), is a popular lunch spot. ⌾ Map E2 • 737 Lamar St, Lincoln Heights • 323-223-1401 • Lunch only • $$

2 Noe
A romantic place for post-theater dining, Noe offers fresh seafood, meats, and poultry prepared in an American-Japanese fusion style. ⌾ Map X4 • 251 S Olive St • 213-356-4100 • $$$$

3 El Tepeyac Café
Lines form outside LA's burrito "headquarters" for the bulging "Hollenbeck," stuffed with guacamole and pork. ⌾ Map E2 • 812 N Evergreen Ave, E LA • 323-267-8668 • No credit cards • $

4 Traxx
This Art Deco restaurant serves classic American dishes with modern touches, such as grilled lamb with pesto farro and goat's cheese. ⌾ Map X4 • 800 N Alameda St • 213-625-1999 • $$

5 Soot Bull Jeep
Grill your own deliciously marinated meat over charcoal at this authentic Korean barbecue place. ⌾ Map D2 • 3136 8th St, Koreatown • 213-387-3865 • $

6 Guelaguetza
This lively restaurant serving food from southern Mexico is famous for its *moles* – sauces made from spices, nuts, chilies, and chocolate. ⌾ Map D2 • 3337 1/2 W 8th St, Koreatown • 213-427-0601 • $

7 Papa Cristo's Taverna
Drop into this friendly, busy eatery next door to St. Sophia (see p83) for fat portions of great Greek food. ⌾ Map D3 • 2771 W Pico Blvd, Koreatown • 323-737-2970 • $

8 El Cholo
This festive Mexican eatery has been full of diners hungry for fajitas and burritos since 1923. Their margaritas pack a wicked punch. ⌾ Map D3 • 1121 S Western Ave, Koreatown • 323-734-2773 • $

9 Taylor's Steakhouse
Send your cholesterol count through the roof at this venerable throwback to the 1950s, with faux leather booths and yummy steaks almost the size of baseball mitts. ⌾ Map D2 • 3361 W 8th St, Koreatown • 213-382-8449 • $$

10 Taix
This 1927 eatery serves value portions of French country classics such as delicious roast chicken with *bordelaise* sauce. Great soups. ⌾ Map E2 • 1911 Sunset Blvd, Echo Park • 213-484-1265 • $$

Unless otherwise stated, all restaurants accept credit cards, serve vegetarian meals, and provide access for the disabled

85

Left **Castle Green, Old Pasadena** Right **The Pasadena Museum of California Art sign**

Pasadena

PASADENA MAY BE CONSIDERED PART OF LA, *but is, in fact, distinctly apart. As LA's first suburb, it attracted a large share of the rich and the powerful who saw to it that a European flair enhanced the town. Fine mansions, such as the masterful Craftsman-era Gamble House, occupy grounds on leafy streets. Old Town Pasadena, the historic core, is now home to a vibrant street with fine restaurants and shops. Pasadena is in the limelight every year on January 1 with its Tournament of Roses, a parade and football game. The area's other treasures include the Rose Bowl and the fabled Huntington Gardens.*

🔟 Sights

1. Huntington Library, Art Collections, & Botanical Gardens
2. Norton Simon Museum
3. Pacific Asia Museum
4. Old Pasadena
5. Rose Bowl
6. Wrigley Mansion & Garden
7. California Institute of Technology
8. Pasadena Civic Center
9. Colorado Street Bridge
10. Pasadena Museum of California Art

Wrigley Mansion & Garden

Stop by the Pasadena Visitors Center located at 171 South Los Robles Avenue

Still Life with Lemons, Oranges, & a Rose by Zurbarán, Norton Simon Museum

Huntington Library, Art Collections, & Botanical Gardens

This treasure trove of high culture is the legacy of railroad baron Henry E. Huntington. He made his vast fortune as a real estate speculator and owner of LA's first mass transit system, the Big Red Cars *(see p25)*.

Norton Simon Museum

This must-see for art lovers owes its existence to Norton Simon, a hugely successful entrepreneur who amassed hundreds of masterpieces *(see p90)* from the Renaissance to the 20th century, and sculpture from India and Southeast Asia. Old Masters such as Rembrandt and Goya and the Impressionists, especially Degas, as well as Renoir, Cézanne, and Monet are well represented. Frank Gehry's remodel improved the lighting conditions of the exhibit space. Sculptures, including Rodin's *The Thinker*, dot the gardens, inspired by Monet's at Giverny in France. Ⓢ *Map E1 • 411 W Colorado Blvd • 626-449-6840 • Open noon– 6pm Wed–Mon, until 9pm Fri • Adm (free for under 19s and students with ID, also on 1st Fri of month) • www.nortonsimon.org*

Pacific Asia Museum

Grace Nicholson, infatuated with all things Asian, had her 1920s private home designed to look like a Chinese imperial palace. It now makes a fitting setting for this museum's artifacts from Asia and the Pacific Islands. Exhibits, usually drawn from the 14,000-strong collection, feature masks from New Guinea, paintings by Japanese masters Hokusai and Hiroshige, and woven costumes from Pakistan. Ⓢ *Map F1 • 46 N Los Robles Ave • 626-449-2742 • Open 10am–6pm Wed–Sun • Adm (free 4th Fri of month) • www.pacificasiamuseum.org*

Old Town Pasadena

Pasadena's historic business district along western Colorado Boulevard was once a decaying part of town, but has now been restored. Today, its handsome brick buildings are packed with boutiques, restaurants, and bookstores. A short detour will take you to the imposing 1898 Castle Green, an apartment building that was once Old Pasadena's most luxurious resort hotel. Ⓢ *Map F1 • Along Colorado Blvd between Marengo Ave & Pasadena Ave • Castle Green, 50 E Green St*

For more on the Huntington Library, Art Collections, & Botanical Gardens See pp22–5

Doo Dah Parade

This over-the-top celebration of wackiness, held every June, began in 1978 as an irreverent spoof of the wholesome Rose Parade. Entrants vary each year but groups such as the Synchronized Precision Briefcase Drill Team and the West Hollywood Transvestite Cheerleaders always generate cheers from the 40,000-strong crowd on Colorado Boulevard.

5 Rose Bowl

Pasadena's most famous landmark, the Rose Bowl draws worldwide attention every New Year's Day when two top-ranking college football teams battle it out for the Rose Bowl Game Trophy. College football first became part of the Tournament of Roses in 1902 when Michigan trounced Stanford 49-0. Architect Myron Hunt's originally horse-shoe-shaped structure was later converted into an elliptical shape and enlarged to its current seating capacity of more than 90,000. Ⓢ Map E1 • 1001 Rose Bowl Dr • 626-577-3101 • www.rosebowlstadium.com

6 Wrigley Mansion & Garden

William Wrigley Jr., the man who gave the world Wrigley's chewing gum, certainly knew how to live. His winter residence in Pasadena is an 18,500-sq-ft (1,720-sq-m) Renaissance-style mansion. It houses the Tournament of Roses Association, which organizes the annual New Year's Day Rose Parade and the Rose Bowl Game. Memorabilia includes Rose Queen crowns, trophies, and photographs. Ⓢ Map E1 • 391 S Orange Grove Blvd • 602-955-4079 • Tours: 10am, noon, 1pm, & 3pm Wed–Sat, 2pm Sun ($15 per person) • Free • www.wrigleymansionclub.com

7 California Institute of Technology (CalTech)

One of the world's leading scientific research centers and a pioneer in earthquake science and molecular biology, CalTech counts 29 Nobel Prize winners among its alumni and faculty, including biologist and current president, David Baltimore. The institute evolved from an arts and crafts school founded in 1891 by the famous Amos G. Throop, changing its focus to science after astronomer George E. Hale became a board member in 1907. Ⓢ Map F2 • 1200 E California Blvd • 626-395-6811 • Campus open anytime • Free guided tours: 10am Mon–Fri (no tours during the winter break & on rainy days) • www.caltech.edu

8 Pasadena Civic Center

This grand complex was inspired by the early 20th-century

Rose Bowl

City Hall, Pasadena Civic Center

City Beautiful movement. It consists of three European-style Beaux-Arts structures stretching along a central axis – the Main Library, the Civic Auditorium, and the City Hall. Architect Myron Hunt designed the public library. Ⓝ Map F1 • City Hall, 100 N Garfield Ave, 626-744-4000 • Civic Auditorium, 300 E Green St, 626-449-7360 • Library, 285 E Walnut St, 626-744-4052

Colorado Street Bridge
The graceful arches of this restored 1913 bridge straddle the Arroyo Seco (Spanish for "dry brook"), a natural ravine that comes down from the San Gabriel Mountains. The imposing 1903 Vista del Arroyo Hotel overlooking the bridge is presently home to the Ninth Circuit Court of Appeals. Ⓝ Map E1 • Court • 125 S Grand Ave • Tours by appointment only • 626-229-7250

Pasadena Museum of California Art
Pasadena art collectors, Robert and Arlene Oltman, occupy the third floor of their 2002 custom-built museum, the only one in the state solely devoted to the art and architecture of California. Water-colors, photographs, and the works of historical as well as living artists are showcased. Ⓝ Map F1 • 490 E Union St • 626-568-3665 • Open noon–5pm Wed–Sun, 5–8pm 3rd Thu of month • Adm (free for under 12s, also on 1st Fri of month) • www.pmcaonline.org

Exploring Historic Pasadena

Morning

A classic way to start the day in Pasadena is with an energizing breakfast at **Marston's** (see p93). After your fill of pancakes, stroll east a couple of blocks on Walnut Street and have a look at the beautiful Beaux-Arts **Main Library** and the majestic **City Hall** a little to the south. Continue farther south to Colorado Boulevard, then head west to **Old Pasadena**, the city's original Downtown, a popular shopping and dining district. Check out the well-restored historic façades while browsing the stores, then pause briefly for a snack at **Café Santorini** (see p93), where you can eat alfresco.

Afternoon

In the afternoon, either drive or walk west along Colorado Boulevard, then turn right on Orange Grove Boulevard to catch the 1pm or 2pm tour of the **Gamble House** (see p91), the Craftsman-era magnum opus by Charles and Henry Greene. Fans of this architectural style could check out several more residences designed by the brothers along nearby Arroyo Terrace and Grand Avenue. Others can make their way back to Colorado Boulevard for a visit to the first-rate **Norton Simon Museum**. The gorgeous gardens are a nice place for a respite and refreshments. A perfect finale to your day is to treat yourself to a grand dinner at **The Raymond** (see p93), one of the city's oldest and most popular restaurants.

Left **Norton Simon Museum** Center **Rembrandt's** *Self-Portrait* Right **Rousseau's** *Exotic Landscape*

TOP 10 Artworks at the Norton Simon Museum

1 Madonna & Child with Book
Renaissance artist Raphael (1483–1520) was only 19 years old when he painted this work. It perfectly exemplifies his geometrically balanced compositions and ability to imbue his figures with spirituality and tenderness.

2 Self-Portrait
No artist has left behind such a thorough record of his own likeness as Rembrandt (1606–69). The elegant garb, dapper beret, and gold chain in this portrait emphasize his social status as a sought-after artist.

3 Still Life with Lemons, Oranges, & a Rose
In this still life, Francisco de Zurbarán (1598–1664) applies the bright colors and minute detail usually reserved for his depictions of saints and clergy.

4 The Triumph of Virtue & Nobility Over Ignorance
Rococo master Giovanni Battista Tiepolo (1696–1770) is known for his exuberant ceiling frescoes. This canvas shows off his bold compositions and use of color.

5 Artist's Garden at Vétheuil
Claude Monet (1840–1926) looked out from his house on the Seine at the sunny, flower-filled garden of this painting.

6 Little Dancer Aged Fourteen
Edgar Degas (1834–1917) was fascinated with dancers, and this exquisite sculpture is one of his finest. The figure is partly painted, dressed in a tulle skirt, and has been given real hair.

7 Portrait of a Peasant
Vincent Van Gogh (1853–90) painted Patience Escalier, a gardener and shepherd, against a night-blue background to create "a mysterious effect, like a star in the depths of an azure sky."

8 Exotic Landscape
Henri Rousseau (1844–1910) is renowned for his poetic, naive paintings that depict magical, lushly landscaped dream worlds. He created this work shortly before his death.

9 Woman with a Book
A highlight of the museum's extensive Picasso (1881–1973) holdings, this graceful painting shows the artist's mistress, Marie-Thérèse Walter, in an introspective mood that contrasts sharply with the melodramatic colors.

10 Shiva & Parvati
This pair of 13th-century Indian bronze sculpture casts depict the Hindu god Shiva, part of the holy Trinity of gods, accompanied by his wife Parvati.

The main floor of this museum showcases European art while the lower galleries display Indian and Southeast Asian art

Left **Tiffany lamp, Gamble House** Center **Charles Sumner Greene House** Right **Halsted House**

TOP10 Greene & Greene Craftsman Houses

The Gamble House (1908)
This handcrafted masterpiece *(see p40)* is a symphony of rich wood, leaded glass windows, and a stained-glass Tiffany door.
⊗ *Map E1 • 4 Westmoreland Place • 626-793-3334 • Tours noon–3pm Thu–Sun • Adm (free for under 12s) • www.gamblehouse.org*

The Cole House (1906)
This large home, owned by a church, marks the first time the Greenes added a *porte-cochere* (a porchlike roof) above the driveway in front of the house.
⊗ *Map E1 • 2 Westmoreland Place*

The Ranney House (1907)
Mary Ranney worked as a draftsperson at the brothers' firm and contributed many of the design ideas for this lovely shingled corner mansion. ⊗ *Map E1 • 440 Arroyo Terrace*

The Hawks House (1906)
This home is distinguished by a very wide covered porch, which keeps out the heat as well as the light, giving the house a rather sombre appearance.
⊗ *Map E1 • 408 Arroyo Terrace*

The Van Rossem-Neill House (1903)
Hemmed in by an unusual wall made of warped clinker bricks and boulders, this pretty house has a stained-glass front door.
⊗ *Map E1 • 400 Arroyo Terrace*

The White Sisters House (1903)
This house has lost much of its Craftsman look thanks to the replacement of the shingle exterior with painted stucco.
⊗ *Map E1 • 370 Arroyo Terrace*

The Charles Sumner Greene House (1901–16)
Charles experimented with many Craftsman ideas while building his own home. The front room, buttressed by boulders and bricks, was a later addition.
⊗ *Map E1 • 368 Arroyo Terrace*

The Duncan-Irwin House (1902)
This large, beautiful home, originally a single story bungalow, pays homage to Japanese design with its slightly upturned roofs.
⊗ *Map E1 • 240 N Grand Ave*

The James Culbertson House (1902–15)
The stained-glass entrance door, the clinker brick wall, and the pergola are the only surviving Greene & Greene elements of this extensively remodeled home. ⊗ *Map E1 • 235 N Grand Ave*

The Halsted House (1905)
Originally one of the brothers' smallest designs, this bungalow sports a deep over-hang of eaves sheltering the main entrance along the drive-way side. ⊗ *Map E1 • 90 N Grand Ave*

 Unless otherwise stated, all the Craftsman Houses are closed to the public

Left **Shops in Old Pasadena** Right **The Lather sign**

🔟 Shopping in Old Pasadena

1 Sur La Table
Cooking aficionados love browsing through this vast assortment of quality kitchenware, from pots and pans to hard-to-find utensils. ⊗ *Map F1 • 161 W Colorado Blvd • 626-744-9987*

2 Restoration Hardware
This retro emporium specializes in reproductions of classic furniture and period hardware such as door knobs, but also has a fun selection of trendy home accessories. ⊗ *Map F1 • 127 W Colorado Blvd • 626-795-7234*

3 Distant Lands Travel Bookstore & Outfitters
A friendly spot packed with travel books, maps, luggage, clothing, and accessories. There is also a travel agency for tickets, tours, and more. ⊗ *Map F1 • 56 S Raymond Ave • 626-449-3220*

4 Lather
This "modern apothecary" uses only natural ingredients for its innovative skin care products and has an assortment of olive oil soap sold by weight. ⊗ *Map F1 • 17 E Colorado Blvd • 626-396-9636*

5 Armani Exchange
This *prêt-à-porter* line by Italian fashion mogul Giorgio Armani is aimed at the client who loves fashionable clothes. It reflects his hallmark simplicity and sophisticated style, but at more affordable prices. ⊗ *Map F1 • 29 W Colorado Blvd • 626-795-7527*

6 Urban Outfitters
Hip, urban clothing, retro and vintage outfits, well-known brands such as Diesel, shoes, gifts, and housewares all under one roof. ⊗ *Map F1 • 139 W Colorado Blvd • 626-449-1818*

7 J. Crew
The retail store of this famous catalog line has the same practical yet stylish clothing and accessories for men and women at reasonable prices. ⊗ *Map F1 • 3 W Colorado Blvd • 626-568-2739*

8 Jumping Jellyfish
This store caters for young children: from infants through to pre-school-age kids. The wide, ever-changing selection of clothes and toys features limited-release lines and clothes from independent designers. ⊗ *Map F1 • Suite 107, 107 S Fair Oaks Ave • 626-578-1838*

9 Apple Store
Everything a Mac enthusiast could want and more. This one-stop shop stocks the latest in Apple technology and has knowledgeable staff on-hand to advise and help with purchases. ⊗ *Map F1 • 54 W Colorado Blvd • 626-577-2685*

10 Gold Bug
This unusual boutique stocks a huge assortment of organic jewelry, artworks, home decor pieces, and other nature-based oddities. ⊗ *Map F1 • 22 E Union St • 626-744-9963*

Price Categories

Price categories include a three-course meal for one, a glass of house wine, and all unavoidable extra charges including tax.

$	under $25
$$	$25–$50
$$$	$50–$80
$$$$	over $80

Left **Parkway Grill** Center **Marston's** Right **Café Santorini**

🔟 Places to Eat

1 Saladang Song
Complex flavors and a lovely Post-Modern patio make this trendy Thai eatery a Pasadena favorite. Insiders swear by the delicious flavored rice soup breakfast. ⌾ *Map F2 • 383 S Fair Oaks Ave • 626-793-5200 • $*

2 Yujean Kang's
Items such as Ants on Tree (glass noodles with flank steak) and Chinese shrimp *polenta* are served in this unusual Chinese restaurant. The wine list is excellent. ⌾ *Map F1 • 67 N Raymond Ave • 626-585-0855 • $$*

3 Marston's
Start the day with blueberry pancakes, golden French toast, or other breakfast favorites at this popular cottage hangout. ⌾ *Map F1 • 151 E Walnut St • 626-796-2459 • Closed Mon • $*

4 The Raymond
One of Pasadena's finest restaurants, this Craftsman-style cottage has a menu of American classics. ⌾ *Map F2 • 1250 S Fair Oaks Ave at Columbia St • 626-441-3136 • Veg: Limited • Closed Mon • $$$*

5 Parkway Grill
Only the freshest organic ingredients are used to perfect inspired Californian cuisine. ⌾ *Map F2 • 510 S Arroyo Parkway • 626-795-1001 • $$*

6 Zankou Chicken
Armenian eatery specializing in chicken *tarna* (chicken with hummus, salad, and garlic sauce), and *shawarma* (meat kebabs). Come hungry. ⌾ *Map F1 • 1296 E Colorado Blvd • 626-405-1502 • $*

7 Bistro 45
This classy place in an Art Deco building turns out excellent French fare paired with one of the best wine lists in town. ⌾ *Map F1 • 45 S Mentor Ave • 626-795-2478 • Veg: Limited • Closed Mon • $$$*

8 Café Santorini
The tables on the terrace are the most coveted on balmy summer evenings. The Greek and Italian menu has lots of fun appetizers. ⌾ *Map F1 • 64 W Union St • 626-564-4200 • No dis. access • $$*

9 Sushi Roku
Classic sushi and creative new takes on Asian food keep this attractively designed place busy. ⌾ *Map F1 • 33 Miller Alley • 626-683-3000 • $$*

10 The Dining Room at The Langham
This formal spot serves experimental food steeped in tradition. Leave room for the Spanish Virgin dessert, a sponge cake served with whipped cream and olive oil ice cream. ⌾ *Map F1 • 1401 S Oak Knoll Ave • 626-585-6218 • $$$*

Unless otherwise stated, all restaurants accept credit cards, serve vegetarian meals, and provide access for the disabled

Left **Hollywood & Highland complex** Right **Paramount Studios entrance**

Hollywood

HOLLYWOOD IS AT ONCE A TOWN, an industry, and an illusion, and you'll experience all of these as you stroll along the famed Hollywood Boulevard. Its history encompasses the birth of the movies, the Golden Age of film premieres, and a crushing decline as the studios moved elsewhere.

Hollywood has since seen a renaissance along the boulevard – the Hollywood and Highland complex is a major development, and many of the grand movie palaces once again host glamorous film openings. At its core, Hollywood is a museum – the huge sign in the hills, movie stars "at your feet" on the Walk of Fame, the bars that hosted greats such as Ernest Hemingway – this is still the place to rekindle childhood dreams about the "stars."

Sights

1. Hollywood Boulevard
2. Hollywood Sign
3. Hollywood Bowl
4. Hollywood Heritage Museum
5. Hollywood Forever Cemetery
6. Paramount Studios
7. Cinerama Dome
8. Crossroads of the World
9. Los Feliz & Silver Lake
10. Hollyhock House

Hollyhock House, designed by Frank Lloyd Wright

For more information on Hollywood, call up the Hollywood Visitors' Information Center at 323-467-6412

Hollywood Boulevard

Hollywood Boulevard

Hollywood's main artery *(see pp 10–11)*, one of the district's most glamorous streets during its pre-World War II heydays, has been revitalized in recent years. The focus of this rejuvenation is the extravagantly designed Hollywood and Highland complex, but old favorites such as TCL Chinese Theatre and the Walk of Fame have also received a fresh sheen. ◈ *Map P2*

Hollywood Sign

From the very beginning, the shiny white Hollywood sign atop Mount Lee was meant to attract attention, originally for the real estate developer and publisher Harry Chandler. Built in 1923 at a cost of $21,000, the sign was once illuminated by 4,000 bulbs and had its own caretaker. Each letter is 50 ft (15 m) tall and is made of sheet metal. In 1932, unemployed actress Peggy Entwistle immortalized herself by leaping to her death off the H. It's illegal to hike to the sign, but the top of Beachwood Drive gets you fairly close to LA's most recognizable landmark. ◈ *Map D2*

Hollywood Bowl

A night at the world's largest natural amphitheater is as much part of Los Angeles summer tradition as backyard barbecues and fun at the beach. The world's finest artists – from Sinatra to Pavarotti – have performed here since 1922. In 1924, Lloyd Wright designed the first concert shell, greatly improving acoustics.
◈ *Map P1 • 2301 N Highland Ave*
• 323-850-2000 • Concerts Tue–Sun late Jun–mid-Sep (tickets required)
• www.hollywoodbowl.com

Hollywood Heritage Museum

This museum is housed in the 1895 barn where Jesse Lasky and Cecil B. De Mille set up Hollywood's first major film studio in 1913. Originally located at Selma Avenue and Vine Street, De Mille shot Hollywood's first full-length feature *The Squaw Man* here in 1913–14. Exhibits include a recreated studio as well as plenty of photographs, props, and memorabilia from the silent movie era. ◈ *Map P1*
• 2100 N Highland Ave • 323-874-2276
• Open noon–4pm Wed–Sun • Adm

Hollywood Sign

Hollywood Sign

Over time the Hollywood Sign lost not only its last four letters (it was originally "Hollywoodland") but also its luster along with the rest of historic Hollywood. A "save-the-sign" campaign in 1978 received the help of celebrities such as Hugh Hefner, who held a fundraiser, and Alice Cooper, who bought the second O in honor of Groucho Marx.

5 Hollywood Forever Cemetery

Founded in 1899, this cemetery has the densest concentration of celebrity corpses in the world. The long list of those interred here includes Rudolph Valentino, Jane Mansfield, and Cecil B. De Mille. The grandest memorial, though, belongs to Douglas Fairbanks Sr. who, since 2000, has shared his marble tomb with his son, Douglas Fairbanks Jr. Buy a map of the graves from the nearby flower shop. ⊗ Map R3 • 6000 Santa Monica Blvd • 323-469-1181 • Open seasonal hours • Free • www.hollywoodforever.com

6 Paramount Studios

The only major movie studio still located in Hollywood, Paramount began making movies with the Paramount logo in 1916. The studio has always had a stunning star roster and in 1929, Paramount's *Wings* took home the first ever Best Picture Oscar. Paramount is well known for successful movies such as *Psycho*, *The Godfather*, *Forrest Gump*, and *Titanic*. Two-hour tours of the studio run Monday to Friday. Under 12s are not permitted. ⊗ Map R4 • 5555 Melrose Ave • 323-956-1777 (reservations required) • Adm

7 Cinerama Dome

A Hollywood landmark and site of many a movie premiere, this white dome of interlocked triangles is LA's most unusual movie theater. The world's only concrete geodesic dome was built by Welton Beckett in 1963 to show Cinerama movies, a revolutionary wide-screen technique requiring three 35 mm projectors. Today, it is part of a modern complex that also includes the ArcLight movie theaters *(see p56)*. ⊗ Map Q3 • 323-464-4226 • www.arclightcinemas.com

8 Crossroads of the World

The centerpiece of this unique architectural metaphor is a shiplike Art Deco building that "sails" into a courtyard flanked by cottages in styles ranging from Spanish Colonial to German

Hollywood Forever Cemetery

For live taping information and reservations at Paramount Studios call 818-753-3470

Crossroads of the World

gingerbread. A quiet office complex, it was built in 1936 by Robert Derrah, who designed Downtown's Coca-Coca Bottling Plant *(see p77)*. ✎ *Map P3 • 6671 Sunset Blvd • Open for strolling*

9 Los Feliz & Silver Lake
The twin neighborhoods of Los Feliz and Silver Lake constitute one of Los Angeles's oldest movie colonies with their bohemian-chic dining, shopping, and nightlife scenes. The hills are studded with architectural Modernist masterpieces such as Frank Lloyd Wright's 1924 Ennis House and the Lovell House built by Richard Neutra. ✎ *Map D2 • Ennis House, 2655 Glendower Ave, closed to the public • Lovell House, 4616 Dundee Dr, closed to the public • Take Red Line to Loz Feliz (Vermont Station)*

10 Hollyhock House
Los Feliz is also home to the Hollyhock House, a community arts center. The Mayan-style mansion was designed by Frank Lloyd in 1921 for oil heiress Aline Barnsdall and has been restored. Depictions of the hollyhock, her favorite flower, appear everywhere on façades and in furniture. ✎ *Map D2 • 4800 Hollywood Blvd • 323-644-6269 • Tours 12:30–3:30pm Wed–Sun • Adm (free for under 13s)*

A Day With the Stars

Morning

Begin at La Brea Avenue and Hollywood Boulevard, heading east to the **Hollywood Roosevelt Hotel** *(see p10 & p146)*, home of the first Academy Awards. In **TCL Chinese Theatre** *(see p11 & p56)* you can stand on the footprints of your favorite stars. An escalator will whisk you into the vast **Hollywood and Highland** complex *(see p11)* with great shopping and views of the **Hollywood Sign** and the dazzling **El Capitan** *(see p56)*. Stop by the **Hollywood Museum** at 1660 N Highland to see costumes, props, and sets from film favorites before taking a two-block detour south on Highland Avenue to **Hollywood High School**, alma mater of Lawrence Fishburne. Have your picture taken with the stars (almost) at **Madame Tussaud's Hollywood**, on 7024 Hollywood Boulevard. From there, head east for a delicious lunch at the **Pig 'n' Whistle** *(see p101)*.

Afternoon

Back on Hollywood Boulevard, you'll come across the exotic **Egyptian Theatre** *(see p11 & p56)* and, at No. 6667, **Musso & Frank Grill** *(see p101)*, Hollywood's oldest restaurant, once the haunt of Chaplin, Hemingway, and other famous people. Wrap up the day with drinks and sunset views at **Yamashiro Restaurant** *(see p100)*, followed by sushi or another Japanese dish at the popular and trendy **Geisha House**, 6633 Hollywood Boulevard. This is also a good spot for celebrity sightings.

Following pages **The brightly lit TCL Chinese Theatre**

Left **A bar in Hollywood** Right **The Cat & Fiddle Pub sign**

🔟 Bars & Dance Clubs

1 Loaded Hollywood
A raucous, gritty dive bar that draws hipsters and fashionistas with its strong drinks, good-looking bartenders, and loud dance music. ⚲ Map Q2 • 6377 Hollywood Blvd • 323-464-5689 • www.loadedhollywood.com

2 Conga Room
Celebrity owners including singer/actor Jennifer Lopez and actor Jimmy Smits bring top salsa and dance acts to this Latin club. ⚲ Map T6 • 800 W Olympic Blvd • 213-749-0445 • www.congaroom.com

3 The Woods
Hidden behind heavy doors in a nondescript mini-mall, this tiki lounge features live bands. ⚲ Map P2 • 1533 N La Brea Ave • 323-876-6612 • www.vintagebargroup.com

4 Boardner's
This unpretentious, historical bar has a lounge with TVs, a patio, live entertainment at night, and a large dance floor in its B52 Club. ⚲ Map P2 • 1652 N Cherokee Ave • 323-462-9621 • www.boardners.com

5 CineSpace
Watch a movie, munch on contemporary American cuisine, and on weekends, listen to a DJ spin house music. ⚲ Map Q2 • 6356 Hollywood Blvd • 323-817-3456 • www.cinespace.info

6 Yamashiro Restaurant
Gorgeous views of the city and sunset cocktails give this Japanese palace an edge. Follow with dinner in the restaurant or enjoy the small garden. ⚲ Map P2 • 1999 N Sycamore Ave • 323-466-5125 • www.yamashirorestaurant.com

7 Create
Top DJs and live electronic music attract large crowds of all ages to the three bars and dance floor. Tickets sell out early, so call ahead. ⚲ Map Q2 • 6021 Hollywood Blvd • 323-463-3331 • www.createnightclub.com

8 Cat & Fiddle Pub
Homesick Brits mingle with midriff-baring LA scenesters. Quaff your libation on the all-Californian patio or beneath the Union Jacks and dartboards inside. Full menu. ⚲ Map Q3 • 6530 Sunset Blvd • 323-468-3800 • www.thecatandfiddle.com

9 Formosa Café
Humphrey Bogart and Marilyn Monroe once hung out at this watering hole. Enjoy the signature mai tais and tasty California-Asian treats. ⚲ Map P3 • 7156 Santa Monica Blvd • 323-850-9050

10 Good Luck Bar
A cool crowd gathers around the oval bar or in the sofa lounge at this fashionable, Chinese-style Silver Lake watering hole. ⚲ Map D2 • 1514 Hillhurst Ave • 323-666-3524

Price Categories

Price categories include a three-course meal for one, a glass of house wine, and all unavoidable extra charges including tax.

$	under $25
$$	$25–$50
$$$	$50–$80
$$$$	over $80

Pig 'n' Whistle

TOP 10 Places to Eat

1 Pig 'n' Whistle
This 1927 landmark has faithfully retained its gorgeous dark wood interior. The menu features famous pork dishes. ✆ *Map P2 • 6714 Hollywood Blvd • 323-463-0000 • Veg: Limited • $$*

2 Franco on Melrose
Enjoy home-made pasta, lamb, linguine with clams, and *carciofi* (raw artichoke salad), as well as delicious desserts, in the romantic outside courtyard setting. BYOB. ✆ *Map N4 • 6919 Melrose Ave • 323-934-3390 • Closed Sun • $$*

3 Ammo
Simple California comfort food is served from morning to night at this tiny but cosy minimalist café. ✆ *Map P3 • 1155 N Highland Ave • 323-871-2666 • $$*

4 Jones Hollywood
Very popular with the locals, this little spot serves classic thin-crust pizza, excellent spaghetti and meatballs, and for many, the best apple pie in town. ✆ *Map N3 • 7205 Santa Monica Blvd • 323-850-1726 • Closed lunch Sat & Sun • $$$$*

5 La Numero Uno
Good place for Mexican specialties like fried plantain with beans and cream, and yucca with *chicharrón* (fried pork rinds). ✆ *Map Q2 • 1247 Vine St • 323-957-1111 • $*

6 Musso and Frank Grill
Steaks and chops dominate the menu of Hollywood's oldest (since 1919) restaurant. It was a major hangout for celebrities such as Hemingway and other literary giants. ✆ *Map P2 • 6667 Hollywood Blvd • 323-467-7788 • $$*

7 Café Stella
This romantic, French-style eatery offers mostly outdoor seating in a lovely courtyard with hanging amber lights and olive and lavender plants. ✆ *Map E2 • 3932 W Sunset Blvd • 323-666-0265 • Closed Sun & Mon • $$*

8 Los Balcones del Peru
This is a casual spot for delicious Peruvian food. Wash it all down with Argentinian wine or Peruvian beer. ✆ *Map Q3 • 1360 Vine St • 323-871-9600 • $$*

9 Madame Matisse
Popular for breakfast, this bistro also turns out delicious French country classics for lunch. BYOB. ✆ *Map D2 • 3536 W Sunset Blvd, Silver Lake • 323-662-4862 • Closed dinner • No dis. access • $*

10 Yuca's Hut
Head this way for yummy Mexican food. Try the *cochinita pibil* tacos. ✆ *Map D2 • 2056 N Hillhurst Ave, Los Feliz • 323-662-1214 • Closed Sun • No credit cards • Veg: No • $*

Unless otherwise stated, all restaurants accept credit cards, serve vegetarian meals, and provide access for the disabled

101

Left **Los Angeles County Museum of Art (LACMA)** Right **Petersen Automotive Museum**

West Hollywood & Midtown

WEST HOLLYWOOD IS LA'S PARTY ZONE *and teems with nightclubs, restaurants, bars, and comedy clubs. After dark, Sunset Strip is the center of the action for poseurs, producers, and the pretty. Huge, lascivious lips on Armani billboards leer down at you, and if you want to be "seen at the scene," this is the place to be. West Hollywood is also LA's "gayest" quarter, especially along Santa Monica Boulevard, where you'll find the party in full swing. For shopaholics there's Melrose Avenue, a quirky pathway lined with designer stores, tattoo parlors, Gothic-chic shops, and bustling cafés and eateries. It's also home to the Pacific Design Center, the anchor of the Avenues of Art & Design, and a treasure trove of chic home accessories. For cultural edification, head south to an amorphous district we've termed "Midtown," whose main artery, Wilshire Boulevard, boasts some of the city's finest museums along the historic Miracle Mile.*

Pacific Design Center (PDC)

🔟 Sights

1. Los Angeles County Museum of Art (LACMA)
2. Farmers Market
3. The Grove
4. Pacific Design Center (PDC)
5. Avenues of Art & Design
6. Melrose Avenue
7. Sunset Strip
8. Petersen Automotive Museum
9. Page Museum & La Brea Tar Pits
10. Craft & Folk Art Museum (CAFAM)

1 Los Angeles County Museum of Art (LACMA)

It's impossible not to marvel when touring the galleries of this well-respected art and culture museum. A virtual cornucopia of paintings, sculpture, furniture, and objects that would take several days to peruse awaits in six buildings. LACMA also hosts international touring exhibits *(see pp16–19)*.

The Theatres sign at The Grove

2 Farmers Market

In 1934, two entrepreneurs asked landowner E.B. Gilmore for permission to start a produce market on a vacant parking lot on his property. Soon after, a group of farmers started selling fresh fruit, flowers, and vegetables from trucks. Many of the 150 stalls of Farmers Market, such as Magee's Nuts, have been in the same families for generations. Scouts from nearby CBS TV City roam the market in search of game show audience members. ✆ Map M5 • 6333 W 3rd St • 323-954-4230 • Open 9am–9pm Mon–Fri, 9am–8pm Sat, 10am–7pm Sun • Free • www.farmersmarketla.com

Farmers Market

3 The Grove

Adjoining the Farmers Market, The Grove is an attractive, upscale outdoor shopping and dining center with a first-rate 14-screen movie theater. This mall features highlights such as a historic trolley connecting it with the market, a fountain that occasionally erupts into a choreographed water show set to music, and a bronze sculpture of flying angels. Along with adjacent CBS Television City and the Farmers Market, The Grove occupies land once owned by the Gilmore family, who made their fortune from oil. Gilmore Stadium, home of the Hollywood Stars, a baseball team owned by Bing Crosby, Cecil B. De Mille, and Barbara Stanwyck, was once located where CBS now stands. ✆ Map N5 • 189 The Grove Drive • 323-900-8000 • Open 10am–9pm Mon–Thu, 10am–10pm Fri & Sat, 10am–8pm Sun

4 Pacific Design Center (PDC)

The 130 showrooms of this vast complex display the finest in furniture, fabrics, lighting, and accessories. A contemporary 1975 design by Cesar Pelli, the most striking feature of the PDC is the gleaming blue glass façade, which has earned it the nickname "The Blue Whale." The clover-green addition dates from 1988. On the plaza behind the PDC is a branch of the Museum of Contemporary Art *(see p72)*, showcasing architecture and design. ✆ Map L4 • 8687 Melrose Ave, 310-657-0800, Open 9am–5pm Mon–Fri, Free • MOCA at PDC, 310-289-5223, Open 11am–5pm Tue–Fri (to 8pm Thu), 11am–6pm Sat & Sun, Free • www.moca.org

The Pacific Design Center tourist office (Suite M-38) is open 9am–5pm Mon–Fri

Gay Los Angeles

West Hollywood is the center of LA's gay and lesbian community. There's plenty of partying in the many happening bars, clubs, cafés, and restaurants along Santa Monica Boulevard. Huge crowds turn up for the colorful Christopher Street West Parade in June and the wonderfully outrageous Halloween Carnival that takes place in late October.

Avenues of Art & Design
The streets surrounding the PDC are flanked with design stores where you can actually buy – and not just look at (as in the PDC) – that chintz sofa or Eames chair. Best explored on foot, the district is filled with cutting-edge art galleries (see p107), trendy restaurants, and cafés where you can relax over latte. ⓢ Map L4 • Along Beverly Blvd, Robertson Blvd, & Melrose Ave between La Cienega Blvd & Doheny Dr

Melrose Avenue
Though it has certainly seen better days, Melrose Avenue (see p108) is still a haven for Hollywood hipsters and the place to stock up on vintage threads, provocative fashions, and unusual gift items. Weekend afternoons are prime time for soaking up the scene, preferably from a table at an outdoor café, delicious ice-cold frappuccino in hand.

Sunset Strip
Sunset Strip has been LA's nocturnal playground since the 1920s and is the most history-laden section of the

Colorful shop window on Melrose Avenue

25-mile (40-km) Sunset Boulevard. Stars, starlets, wannabes, and those that like to be around them are still drawn to landmarks old and new, including the Chateau Marmont, the Whisky a Go-Go, the Mondrian Hotel with its exclusive Sky Bar, and Johnny Depp's music club, the Viper Room (see pp8–9).

Petersen Automotive Museum
LA's evolution from sleepy outpost to sweeping megalopolis is uniquely tied to the rise of the automobile. This is the basic premise of this wonderful museum, which does a lot more than display pretty vintage cars (though there are plenty of those, too). On the ground floor, you'll follow a Los Angeles "streetscape" through 100 years of car history. You'll pass dioramas of a 1920s gas station, a 1930s showroom, and a 1950s drive-in restaurant. Upstairs, the cars take center stage. Exhibits change regularly, but usually include galleries devoted to hot rods, motorcycles, and vehicles owned by Hollywood celebrities or used in movies. For children, the Discovery Center makes science fun. ⓢ Map M6 • 6060 Wilshire Blvd, Miracle Mile • 323-930-2277 • Open 10am–6pm Tue–Sun • Adm

Page Museum at the La Brea Tar Pits
Mammoths, saber-toothed cats, and dire wolves are the stars of this museum offering a look at life in LA during the last Ice Age thousands of years ago. Since

The Pit 91 Visitors Station (La Brea Tar Pits) is open 10am–4pm daily during summer; entry is free

La Brea Tar Pits

1906, excavations at the pits adjacent to the museum have yielded more than one million fossilized bones of about 450 species, from insects to birds and mammals. Many are now on display at the museum, which also houses a glass-walled laboratory where paleontologists may be seen working. Outside the museum, life-size replicas of mammoths trapped in muck dramatize the ghastly fate of Los Angeles's prehistoric denizens.
🔊 *Map N6 • 5801 Wilshire Blvd, Miracle Mile • 323-934-7243 • Open daily • Adm (free first Tue of month and for under 5s) • www.tarpits.org*

10 Craft & Folk Art Museum (CAFAM)

This small museum is dedicated to showcasing handicrafts and folk art from around the world. The brainchild of folk art collector Edith Wyle, it was originally launched in 1965 as "The Egg and The Eye," a gallery space and omelet restaurant. Apart from its changing exhibits, which reflect the multi-layered culture of Southern California, CAFAM is best known for its annual International Festival of Masks held in October.
🔊 *Map N6 • 5814 Wilshire Blvd, Miracle Mile • 323-937-4230 • Open 11am–5pm Tue–Fri, noon–6pm Sat & Sun • Adm (free 1st Wed of month and for under 10s) • www.cafam.org*

A Day in Hollywood

Morning

🕐 Start your day at Wilshire Boulevard's "Museum Row" to catch the latest headline exhibit at **LACMA** *(see pp16–19)* or selections from its superb permanent collection. Don't miss the beautiful Pavilion for Japanese Art. If you can muster the energy before lunch, head for the **Petersen Automotive Museum** or the **Page Museum**.

Leaving Museum Row, drive a few blocks north to the **Farmers Market**. Try the Cajun food at **Gumbo Pot**, the all-American menu at the retro **Kokomo Café**, or the **Du-Par's** diner fare.

Afternoon

For an afternoon of shopping, start with the Farmers Market itself, then wander over to **The Grove**, an outdoor mall. Head north on Fairfax Avenue, turning right on **Melrose Avenue**. This quintessential LA shopping street is packed with fun and funky stores and offers great people-watching opportunities, especially on weekends.

Head for an early dinner at **Echigo** *(see p109)*, where you'll be treated to delicious, traditional-style sushi, then drive to **Sunset Strip** for an evening of laughs at the **Comedy Store** *(see p55)* or **The Laugh Factory** *(see p55)*. Make your reservations in advance. Showtime is usually 8pm. Round off your day with a drink at **Bar Marmont** *(see p106)* or the lounge at the chic **Standard Hollywood** *(see p147)*.

Left **House of Blues** Right **The Roxy sign**

Sunset Strip Bars & Clubs

1 Bar Marmont
Super-trendy lounge next to the Chateau Marmont hotel with lots of beautiful people to gawk at. To increase your chances of getting past the front door arrive early, by about 9 or 10pm. ✆ *Map M3 • 8171 Sunset Blvd • 323-650-0575*

2 Hyde Lounge
Glamour, excess, and an A-list clientele are assured at this LA hot spot. The intimate setting means space is limited so arrive early to ensure entry. ✆ *Map M3 • 8029 W Sunset Blvd • 323-656-4933*

3 The Cactus Lounge at the Standard
The entertainment at this hotel hot spot includes a live acoustic music series, book readings, a DJ above the reception, and dancing. ✆ *Map M3 • 8300 Sunset Blvd • 323-822-3111*

4 House of Blues
The original HOB branch has an eclectic schedule of performers, including long-time favorites such as Joan Armatrading and the Bangles. The Sunday Gospel brunch is an institution. ✆ *Map M3 • 8430 Sunset Blvd • 323-848-5100*

5 Sky Bar
Famous for its poolside cocktails, celebrity crowd, and sweeping city views, getting past the velvet rope here is a tall order. ✆ *Map M3 • 8440 Sunset Blvd, at the Mondrian Hotel • 323-848-6025*

6 Saddle Ranch Chop House
A Texas-style steakhouse popular with families until 10pm, after which it becomes a lively night-time hangout. ✆ *Map M3 • 8371 W Sunset Blvd • 323-656-2007*

7 Viper Room
Celebrity musicians such as Bruce Springsteen stage concerts at this club, once owned by Johnny Depp *(see p9 & p64)*. ✆ *Map L3 • 8852 Sunset Blvd • 310-358-1880*

8 Whisky a Go-Go
LA's epicenter of rock'n'roll in the 1960s, this club was the springboard for the Doors and still books new bands. ✆ *Map L3 • 8901 W Sunset Blvd • 310-652-4202*

9 The Roxy
Serious music fans love this no-nonsense club where the focus is on the show, not the decor or the crowd. ✆ *Map K3 • 9009 W Sunset Blvd • 310-278-9457*

10 The Cutting Room
This lounge, with black leather couches and red walls covered with rock albums, offers beer and imaginative cocktails. ✆ *Map M3 • 8462 W Sunset Blvd • 323-650-1250*

Left **The Margo Leavin Gallery sign** Right **George Stern Fine Arts**

TOP 10 Art Galleries

1 Margo Leavin Gallery
Margo Leavin presents contemporary American and European art and photography. Claes Oldenburg designed the sculpture "Knife Slicing Through Water" by the entrance. ✆ Map L4
• 812 N Robertson Blvd • 310-273-0603

2 Gallery 1988
This small space is crowded with some of the city's hottest new talent. It's become known as the best place in the country for pop-culture-themed work and draws as many as 2,500 people for opening events. ✆ Map K4
• 7010 Melrose Ave • 323-937-7088

3 George Stern Fine Arts
This gallery specializes in late 19th and early 20th-century California-based Impressionist landscape painters such as Guy Rose and Maurice Brown. ✆ Map K4 • 8920 Melrose Ave • 310-276-2600

4 Tasende Gallery
Modern and contemporary sculpture, drawings as well as paintings by international artists such as Eduardo Chillida or Henry Moore are on view. ✆ Map L4 • 8808 Melrose Ave • 310-276-8686

5 Hamilton-Selway Gallery
Home to the largest collection of Andy Warhol originals on the West Coast, this gallery also features Roy Lichtenstein, Keith Haring, and other pop art icons. ✆ Map L4
• 8678 Melrose Ave • 310-657-1711

6 Tobey C. Moss
This LA art scene fixture began with a focus on prints and drawings, but is best known as a keen promoter of pre-1960s California Modernists. ✆ Map N5
• 7321 Beverly Blvd • 323-933-5523

7 Regen Projects
This unassuming space, hidden in an alley, presents cutting-edge contemporary art by emerging and established artists, such as Catherine Opie, Lari Pittman, and Richard Prince. ✆ Map K4 • 633 N Almont Dr • 310-276-5424

8 Known Gallery
Specializing in contemporary, "street", and graffiti artists, the monthly exhibitions at this spacious and welcoming gallery draw large crowds. ✆ Map M4
• 441 N Fairfax Ave • 310-860-6263
• www.knowngallery.com

9 Fahey/Klein Gallery
A power in the world of rare, vintage, and contemporary art photography, Fahey/Klein showcases Henri Cartier-Bresson and other high-profile artists. ✆ Map P5 • 148 N La Brea Ave • 323-934-2250

10 Jan Baum Gallery
Jan Baum is a top dealer in international and American art and represents prominent African-American artists, including the Saar family. Betye Saar designed Downtown's Biddy Mason park (see p78). ✆ Map P5
• 170 S La Brea Ave • 323-932-0170

Left **Melrose Trading Post** Center & Right **Off the Wall Antiques sign & shop**

🔟 Shops on Melrose Avenue

1 Bodhi Tree Bookstore
This esoteric bookstore specializes in New Age topics such as mysticism and astrology. Browse the shelves or attend lectures; you can even consult the resident psychic. ✎ *Map L4* • *8585 Melrose Ave • 310-659-1733*

2 Decades & Decades Two
If Rodeo Drive is out of your league, try this couture resale boutique. Downstairs you'll find lightly worn clothing, while upstairs stocks 1960s and 1970s Pucci and Courrèges. ✎ *Map M4* • *8214 Melrose Ave • 323-655-1960*

3 Fred Segal
This über-trendy house of style attracts A-list celebrities. Shop for fashionable clothes, luxurious beauty products, and gift items at steep prices *(see p64)*. ✎ *Map M4 • 8100 Melrose Ave (also at 420 Broadway, 500 Broadway)* • *323-651-4129, 310-394-9814*

4 Melrose Trading Post
This cool Sunday flea market takes you back through the years with vintage fashions, collectibles, and retro furnishings. ✎ *Map M4* • *At the corner of Melrose & Fairfax Aves* • *323-655-7679 • Open 9am–5pm Sun* • *Adm (free for under 12s)*

5 Wasteland
Stylists and bargain-hunters shop for vintage clothing, accessories, and shoes at this warehouse-sized store. ✎ *Map N4* • *7428 Melrose Ave • 323-653-3028*

6 Wanna Buy a Watch?
Best known for its selection of vintage watches, this classy store now stocks contemporary watch models, antique diamond rings, and 1920s Art Nouveau baubles as well. ✎ *Map N4* • *8465 Melrose Ave • 323-653-0467*

7 LA Eyeworks
This unusual and happening store is known for featuring the most unique eyeglass designs on the planet and attracts its share of the hip crowd. ✎ *Map N4* • *7407 Melrose Ave • 323-653-8255*

8 Maya Jewelry
This small store stocks affordable jewelry, mostly silver, to adorn any body part you wish to, including toes, tongues, and belly buttons. Also has a great mask collection. ✎ *Map N4* • *7452 Melrose Ave • 323-655-2708*

9 Fitzsu Society
Seeking to promote better living through better design, Fitzsu Society stocks an eclectic mix of contemporary furniture, housewares, and gifts by well-known international designers such as Phillippe Starck. ✎ *Map N4* • *7970 Melrose Ave • 323-655-1908*

10 Off the Wall Antiques
There's plenty of kitsch with classic neon signs, vintage toys, Art Deco lamps, and various other collectibles at this emporium of weird Americana. ✎ *Map N4 • 7325 Melrose Ave • 323-930-1185*

Price Categories

Price categories include a three-course meal for one, a glass of house wine, and all unavoidable extra charges including tax.

$	under $25
$$	$25–$50
$$$	$50–$80
$$$$	over $80

M Café de Chaya

🔟 Places to Eat

1 Angelini Osteria
Having cooked for the Pope and presidents, Chef Angelini now regales homesick Italians and foodies with his comfort food. ◈ *Map N5 • 7313 Beverly Blvd • 323-297-0070 • Veg: On request • Closed Mon • $$*

2 Swingers
This retro diner with its plaid booths and Andy Warhol wallpaper serves steamy chicken soup and bulging sandwiches until the wee hours. ◈ *Map M5 • 8020 Beverly Blvd • 323-653-5858 • $*

3 Animal
An influential place in the LA dining scene, the food here is rich, indulgent, and carnivore-friendly. Try the chicken-liver mousse or smoked trout salad. ◈ *Map M4 • 435 N Fairfax • 323-782-9225 • $$$*

4 Joan's on Third
This little deli is great for gourmets on the go or out for a casual lunch. The tarragon chicken salad is excellent. ◈ *Map M5 • 8350 W 3rd St • 323-655-2285 • $*

5 The Palm
A West Hollywood fixture since 1975, this steakhouse is famous for its generous portions. Caricatures of the stars line the walls. ◈ *Map L3 • 9001 Santa Monica Blvd • 310-550-8811 • $$$*

6 Lucques
Try the short ribs, duck confit, and pancetta-wrapped trout at this intimate spot. Enjoy the desserts with an after-dinner drink by the fireplace. ◈ *Map N4 • 8474 Melrose Ave • 323-655-6277 • $$$$*

7 M Café de Chaya
Chaya's macrobiotic cuisine has a huge following. Try an exquisite salad or club sandwich with tempeh "bacon." ◈ *Map P4 • 7119 Melrose Ave • 323-525-0588 • $$*

8 Newsroom Café
The patio provides premier celeb-watching, and the eclectic menu brims with low-fat and vegan options. ◈ *Map L5 • 120 N Robertson Blvd • 310-652-4444 • $*

9 Echigo
Sushi of all types and stripes is on offer, and all of it is fresh. Ask the chef for the daily specialty. ◈ *Map R3 • 12217 Santa Monica Blvd • 310-820-9787 • Closed Sun • $$$$*

10 The Ivy
Join the stars in two dining rooms filled with flowers. Try the Caesar salad or the plump and crispy crab cakes. ◈ *Map L4 • 113 N Robertson Blvd • 310-274-8303 • $$$*

Unless otherwise stated, all restaurants accept credit cards, serve vegetarian meals, and provide access for the disabled

109

Left **The Paley Center for Media** Right **Beverly Hills City Hall, Civic Center**

Beverly Hills, Westwood, & Bel-Air

STAFF IN LIVERY STANDING OVER ROWS *of rolls royces, Tom Cruise disembarking from a stretch limo, cellphone-addicted fat-cat producers cutting poolside deals in pleasure-palace hotels, slinky young things in black – this is Beverly Hills where the smell of money drapes the very breeze. But there is more than just opulence and wealth here. Adjacent Westwood is home to UCLA, one of the finest public universities in the country. The nearby Getty Center serenely lords above it all in its white majesty. Bel Air mansions have routinely passed from Fairbanks and Bogart to Streisand and Diaz. Beverly Hills and its environs offer glimpses into a fairytale lifestyle unattainable for most.*

Rodeo Drive

Beverly Hills Hotel

You'll often spot nicely groomed shoppers, though actual star sightings are rare. Rodeo's southern end is punctuated by the Four Seasons Beverly Wilshire, one of LA's grandest hotels *(see p144)*. Architecture fans check out Frank Lloyd Wright's Anderton Court *(see p114)*. ✆ *Rodeo Drive between Wilshire & Santa Monica Blvds*

3 The Paley Center for Media

Most people alive today have grown up watching television, one of the defining media of the 20th century. This center, housed in a striking building by Getty Center architect Richard Meier, was originally built to collect, preserve, and share nearly 80 years of radio and TV history. About 120,000 programs – news to musicals, sports to sitcoms – have been catalogued and are available for viewing and listening. Today it has expanded to include resources for digital media and offers a wide schedule of classes and events. ✆ *Map J5 • 465 N Beverly Dr • 310-786-1000 • Open noon–5pm Wed–Sun • Donation • www.paleycenter.org*

4 Beverly Hills Civic Center

The wealth of a city is often reflected in its public buildings, so it should come as no surprise that Beverly Hills has the kind of civic center that's the envy of other towns. Its centerpiece is the elegant City Hall, built in 1932 in Spanish Renaissance style and harmoniously incorporated into a contemporary Spanish-style complex with palm-lined walkways and curved colonnades. It houses a beautiful library as well as the local police and fire departments. ✆ *Map J5 • East of Crescent Dr between Santa Monica Blvd & Burton Dr*

1 Beverly Hills Hotel

LA's most famous hotel *(see p146)* has been part of Hollywood history since its 1912 opening. Douglas Fairbanks Sr. and Will Rogers got drunk in the bar, Howard Hughes rented Bungalow 3 for 30 years, and Marilyn Monroe reportedly romanced both JFK and RFK here. Political leaders, royals, and Hollywood headliners have all stayed, partied, and cavorted at the legendary Pink Palace. It's been featured in movies and on the cover of the Eagles' *Hotel California* album. And stars still come – Elton John celebrated his 55th birthday here in 2002. ✆ *Map J4 • 9641 Sunset Blvd • 310-276-2251 • www.beverlyhillshotel.com*

2 Rodeo Drive

Rodeo Drive *(see p52 & p114)* is one of the world's most famous – and expensive – shopping streets, synonymous with a lifestyle of luxury and fame. Only three blocks long, it is essentially an haute couture runway, with all the major international players represented.

Beverly Hills by Numbers

Wealthy Beverly Hills still surprises in some aspects. Its well-heeled denizens are – two to one – registered Democrats. They really love their kids and spend 28% more every year than the state's average to educate them. And with an unemployment rate near 3%, these natives continue raking in their average $65,507 per capita incomes.

5 Museum of Tolerance

This high-tech museum confronts visitors with issues of extreme intolerance to make them realize the need for greater acceptance in today's world. The experience begins at the "Tolerancenter," whose exhibits address issues such as human rights violations and the Civil Rights movement. The Holocaust section, at the core, chronicles Nazi atrocities. A multimedia exhibit follows the lives of well-known Americans from different ethnic backgrounds. Ⓢ *Map D2*
• *9786 W Pico Blvd* • *310-772-2505*
• *Open 10am–5pm Mon–Fri, 11am–5pm Sun (Nov–Mar: till 3pm Fri); Closed Jewish holidays.* • *Reservations only*
• *Adm* • *www.museumoftolerance.com*

6 University of California, Los Angeles (UCLA)

One of the nation's top research universities, UCLA (founded in 1919) counts many luminaries among its alumni, including Francis Ford Coppola. It has around 150 buildings, with architectural gems such as Royce Hall. The Fowler Museum has a marvellous collection of non-Western art. To the north is the lovely Franklin D. Murphy Sculpture Garden *(see p43)*.
Ⓢ *Map C2* • *Bounded by Sunset Blvd & Le Conte, Hilgard, & Gayley Aves* • *310-825-4321* • *www.ucla.edu*

7 UCLA Hammer Museum

This museum, run by UCLA, is the legacy of Armand Hammer, an oil tycoon who discovered a passion for collecting art in the 1920s. Hammer was especially fond of 19th-century French Impressionists such as Monet. Rotating exhibitions are complemented by traveling shows with a more contemporary angle. Free readings, film screenings, and lectures are quite popular. Phone ahead or check the website for the latest events and exhibits. Ⓢ *Map C2*
• *10899 Wilshire Blvd* • *310-443-7000*
• *Open 11am–8pm Tue–Fri, 11am–5pm Sat & Sun* • *Adm (free for under 17s, free for students with ID, free Thu)* • *www.hammer.ucla.edu*

8 Pierce Brothers Westwood Village Memorial Park

This small cemetery beneath Westwood's towering office high-rises has more Hollywood stars per square yard than any other burial ground in LA. Marilyn Monroe's remains rest in an above-ground crypt always decorated with flowers (Hugh Hefner has allegedly reserved the adjacent space). Other celebs buried here are Burt Lancaster, Natalie Wood, and Frank Zappa.
Ⓢ *Map C2* • *1218 Glendon Ave* • *310-474-1579* • *Open 8am–sunset*

Entrance to UCLA Hammer Museum

The Fowler Museum at UCLA is open noon–5pm Wed–Sun (until 8pm Thu); entry is free

Skirball Cultural Center

Skirball Cultural Center

This state-of-the-art Jewish cultural center was named after its main benefactor, Jack Skirball (1896–1985), a rabbi and producer of Hitchcock films. The complex hosts a lively events schedule and has a multimedia museum. Exhibits explore the parallels between the Jewish experience and the principles of American democracy. The center's ongoing exhibition, *Visions and Values*, looks at Jewish life from Antiquity to America. ✆ *Map C2 • 2701 N Sepulveda Blvd, Brentwood/Bel-Air • 310-440-4500 • Open noon–5pm Tue–Fri, 10am–5pm Sat & Sun • Adm (free for under 2s, free Thu) • www.skirball.org*

The Getty Center

Although best known for its collection of European art, the Getty offers much more – a hilltop setting with sweeping views from the ocean to the mountains, architecture as exquisite as "frozen music" (to quote Goethe), and landscaped gardens that are nothing less than the finest art *(see pp12–15)*.

Tour of Stars' Homes

Morning

🕐 Begin your tour of stars' homes by driving north on Walden Drive, just off Santa Monica Boulevard, for a glimpse of **"Witch's House"** at the corner of Carmelita Avenue, famous for its Hansel-and-Gretel looks. Go right on Lomitas Avenue, then left on Linden Drive where mobster Bugsy Siegel was gunned down at **No. 810** in 1947. Follow Linden north to Sunset Boulevard, turn right, then left on Roxbury Avenue for two star-packed blocks. Apart from Jimmy Stewart, who lived at **No. 918**, you'll also see the former homes of song lyricist Ira Gershwin (**No. 1021**), Diane Keaton (**No. 1025**), singer Rosemary Clooney (aunt of George, at **No. 1019**), Peter Falk (**No. 1004**), comedian Jack Benny (**No. 1002**), and Lucille Ball (**No. 1000**).

Turn right on Cañon Drive, then right again on Bedford Drive where the house at **No. 904** was at different times the homes of stars such as Frank Sinatra, Rex Harrison, Anthony Quinn, Greta Garbo, and Ava Gardner. Steve Martin used to live at **No. 721** and Lana Turner at **No. 730**. It was here in 1958 that Lana's daughter Cheryl Crane is believed to have killed her mother's mobster-lover Johnny Stompanato. At **No. 512** is the former home of silent screen siren Clara Bow where, in 1927, she was rumored to have "entertained" the entire USC football team, including Marion Morrison, better known by his screen name of John Wayne.

Left **Two Rodeo** Center **The Tiffany & Co sign** Right **Lalique lamp**

Temptations on Rodeo Drive

Two Rodeo
This cobbled lane resembles an idealized European shopping avenue with fountains, street lamps, and a piazza. When it opened in 1990, it was the first new street in Beverly Hills since 1914. ✆ Map J6
• Rodeo Dr at Wilshire Blvd

Tiffany & Co
The meticulously crafted jewelry is as exquisite as Audrey Hepburn was in the movie *Breakfast at Tiffany's,* based on the famous store in New York. ✆ Map J5 • 210 N Rodeo Dr • 310-273-8880

A Gucci cushion

Lalique
Best known for its exquisite crystal pieces, this boutique actually stocks the entire product line, including jewelry, watches, and perfume. ✆ Map J5 • 238 N Rodeo Dr • 310-271-7892

David Orgell
A Rodeo Drive fixture since 1958, this luxury emporium is famous for its antique silver, unique jewelry, and limited edition designer watches. ✆ Map J5 • 320 N Rodeo Dr • 310-273-6660

Anderton Court
One of Frank Lloyd Wright's later buildings (1953), the zig-zagging ramp cradling a well of light is reminiscent of the New York Guggenheim Museum. ✆ Map J5 • 333 N Rodeo Dr

Gucci
The store is a sure-fire winner in the looks department, but most customers have eyes only for the trademark shoes, handbags, and accessories. ✆ Map J5 • 347 N Rodeo Dr • 310-278-3451

Harry Winston
On Oscar night, when the stars come out dripping with diamonds, they're most likely on loan from the family-owned Harry Winston, one of the world's most exclusive jewelers. ✆ Map J5 • 310 N Rodeo Dr • 310-271-8554

Bijan
This boutique stocks quality menswear, said to be the world's most expensive. Client names from Prince Charles to Steven Spielberg are etched into the window. ✆ Map J5 • 420 N Rodeo Dr • 310-273-6544 • Open by appointment

The Rodeo Collection
A white marble outdoor shopping mall with five floors of fashion, interior design, and jewelry boutiques orbiting a sunken atrium courtyard with a fancy eatery. ✆ Map J5 • 421 N Rodeo Dr

O'Neill House
Completed in 1988, this complex sports whimsical Art Nouveau design elements borrowed from Catalan architect Antonio Gaudí. ✆ Map J5 • 507 N Rodeo Dr • Not open to the public

Price Categories

Price categories include a three-course meal for one, a glass of house wine, and all unavoidable extra charges including tax.

$ under $25
$$ $25–$50
$$$ $50–$80
$$$$ over $80

Crustacean

Places to Eat

1 Spago Beverly Hills

Stargazers are likely to report sightings when dining at Wolfgang Puck's flagship restaurant, one of the pioneers of California cuisine. ® Map K5 • 176 N Cañon Dr • 310-385-0880 • $$$

2 Crustacean

A Beverly Hills hot spot, this French Colonial restaurant serves refined Vietnamese cuisine. Try anything made with owner/chef's "secret spices." ® Map J5 • 9646 S Santa Monica Blvd • 310 205-8990 • $$$

3 Kate Mantalini

This busy upscale diner in the heart of Beverly Hills serves standard American fare including chicken pot pie, meatloaf and power breakfasts. ® Map K6 • 9101 Wilshire Blvd • 310-278-3699 • $$

4 Polo Lounge

The menu of this Beverly Hills Hotel restaurant mixes signature dishes such as McCarthy salad with healthy Asian and hearty California cuisine. ® Map J4 • 9641 Sunset Blvd • 310-276-2251 • Veg: On request • $$

5 Belvedere

Hollywood power brokers love the gold and peach dining room and impeccable service here. The creative menu changes with the seasons. ® Map J5 • 9882 Santa Monica Blvd • 310-788-2306 • $$$

6 Natalee Thai

Peruse the entertaining menu, then choose from various Thai classics that are served family-style. ® Map L6 • 998 S Robertson Blvd (also at 10101 Venice Blvd, Culver City) • 310-855-9380 • $

7 Matsuhisa

This is the original of Nobu Matsuhisa's small but growing empire of Japanese-Peruvian seafood restaurants. Ignore the menu and surrender to the chef's imagination. ® Map L5 • 129 N La Cienega Blvd • 310-659-9639 • $$$

8 Nate'n Al

This modest kosher deli has been catering to the stars since 1943. Regulars swear by the huge sandwiches served on chunky rye bread. ® Map J5 • 414 N Beverly Dr • 310-274-0101 • $

9 Xi'an

For a light and tasty take on classic Chinese dishes, head to this stylish place with an outdoor patio. Try the marvelous black bean sauce and the Peking duck. ® Map J5 • 362 N Cañon Dr • 310-275-3345 • $$

10 Il Cielo

Book a romantic table beneath a star-lit sky in the enchanting garden and enjoy the classic and delicious fare. ® Map K5 • 9018 Burton Way • 310-276-9990 • Closed Sun • $$

Around Town – Beverly Hills, Westwood, & Bel-Air

Unless otherwise stated, all restaurants accept credit cards, serve vegetarian meals, and provide access for the disabled

115

Left **Entrance to Santa Monica Pier** Center **Venice Boardwalk** Right **Venice Canal**

Santa Monica Bay

*S*ANTA MONICA BAY SPANS ABOUT *20 miles (32 km) between two of the richest communities in California – Malibu and Palos Verdes. It's truly the "Gold Coast" of the Golden State, and its shores have some of the finest beaches anywhere, including Topanga, Santa Monica, and Venice on through Manhattan, Hermosa, Redondo, and Torrance. American surfing, and the youth culture it spawned, was born here. In the movies, these fabled beaches have stood in for everything from Guadalcanal and Tahiti to Shangri-la. The rows of mammoth palms along the Santa Monica promenade cliffs epitomize California. Access to the Pacific along the beaches – whether by ferry to Catalina Island, surfing, taking a gondola cruise through the canals of Long Beach, or just popping into the local waves from a newly discovered favorite strand – is bountiful. Take the plunge! Santa Monica's main attraction, however, is Santa Monica Pier, which offers sundry entertainment options and a lively carnival atmosphere.*

🔟 Sights

1. **Malibu Adamson House**
2. **Santa Monica Pier**
3. **Bergamot Station Arts Center**
4. **Third Street Promenade**
5. **Venice Boardwalk**
6. **Venice Canals**
7. **Marina del Rey**
8. **South Bay**
9. **Palos Verdes Peninsula**
10. **Wayfarer's Chapel**

Malibu Adamson House

1 Malibu Adamson House

Located on a bluff overlooking the Malibu Lagoon, this Spanish Colonial-style mansion was built by Rhoda Rindge Adamson and her husband, Merritt, in 1928. The complex showcases hand-painted ceramic tiles manufactured by Malibu Potteries, owned by the Rindge family. The Rindges also built the Malibu Colony, a celebrity enclave now home to Tom Hanks and Barbra Streisand. The Malibu Lagoon Museum next to the Adamson House chronicles Malibu's history, from its Chumash Indian origins to its position as movie star Shangri-la. ✪ Map A3 • 23200 Pacific Coast Hwy, Malibu, 310-456-8432 • Adamson House, Open 11am–3pm Wed–Sat (last tour 2pm), Adm (cash only) • Malibu Lagoon Museum, Open 11am–3pm, Adm (free for under 18s)

Intricate tile detail in Adamson House

2 Santa Monica Pier

For a variety of entertainment, visit Santa Monica Pier. Where else can you hop on to a historic carousel, visit an aquarium, or ride a roller coaster? California's oldest amusement pier (built in 1908) also marks the western terminus of Route 66. Its oldest attraction is the 1922 Looff Hippodrome, a carousel that has made many movie appearances. It is located in Pacific Park, a compact amusement park anchored by a solar-powered Ferris wheel. Tucked beneath the pier, the Santa Monica Pier Aquarium is a small, family-oriented facility where you can observe and pet local marine life. ✪ Map A4 • At the end of Colorado Ave • Hippodrome, 310-394-8042, Open 11am–5pm daily (to 7pm Fri–Sun) • Pacific Park, 310-260-8744 • Santa Monica Pier Aquarium, 310-393-6149

3 Bergamot Station Arts Center

This former historic trolley station has been imaginatively recycled into an industrial-flavored complex of nearly three dozen galleries, shops, artists' studios, and a café. A highlight is the Santa Monica Art Museum, exhibiting cutting-edge artists, many of whom work in non-traditional media including video installations. It also organizes lectures, workshops, and other events designed to involve the community in the creative process. ✪ Map B4 • 2525 Michigan Ave, Santa Monica, 310-586-6488 • Santa Monica Museum of Art, Open 11am–6pm Tue–Sat, Donation, www.smmoa.org • Other galleries, Open 10am–6pm Tue–Fri, 11am–5:30pm Sat, Free

4 Third Street Promenade

Downtown Santa Monica's main artery, this three-block mall is one of the most pleasant walking areas in LA. The product

Poster on display in Bergamot Station

The "Father of Venice"

Venice sprang from the vision of tobacco magnate Abbot Kinney (1850–1920), who transformed the soggy marshland lying south of Santa Monica into a canal-laced, oceanfront theme park complete with gondolas and an amusement pier. It opened on July 4, 1905, and was a grand success until fire destroyed most of the theme park facilities in 1920.

of a hugely successful revitalization effort in the late 1980s, it is flanked by upscale shops, movie theaters, and eclectic restaurants, bars, and cafés. Street musicians from around the globe perform flamenco, jazz, and hip hop. On Wednesday and Saturday mornings, the farmers market attracts large crowds. Ⓢ *Map A4 • 3rd St between Broadway & Wilshire Blvd, Santa Monica*

Venice Boardwalk

It is perhaps fitting that Venice Beach, masterminded by an eccentric visionary named Abbot Kinney *(see box)*, is LA's epicenter of counterculture. The circus-like scene reigning along the seaside boardwalk (officially known as "Ocean Front Walk") must be seen to be believed *(see p122)*. Avoid after dark. Ⓢ *Map A5 • Ocean Front Walk between Venice Blvd & Rose Ave*

Venice Canals

Abbot Kinney's Venice of America was once laced with 16 miles (26 km) of canals. The area languished until the 1960s when beatniks such as Stuart Perkoff discovered its unique charm, dragging flower children – most famously Jim Morrison – in their wake. In 1994, the city restored 3 miles (5 km) of canals, which have since become a beautiful,

upscale neighborhood. A narrow walkway that is known as the Venice Canal Walk threads through here. Ⓢ *Map A6 • Between Washington & Venice Blvds*

Marina del Rey

With over 6,000 yachts and pleasure boats, Marina del Rey is the largest small-craft harbor in the world and the place to come for those seeking fun on the water. Active types could explore the harbor on kayaks. You can also catch a dinner cruise, book a whale-watching trip (January to March), or charter a sport fishing boat. Favorite landlubber activities include a sunset dinner at one of the many excellent restaurants. Ⓢ *Map C3 • South of Venice Beach • Visitors Bureau • 4701 Admiralty Way • 310-305-9545*

South Bay

Surfing, swimming, tanning, beach volleyball, and other outdoor pursuits govern the laid-back lifestyle of the string of three picture-perfect beach towns in the southern Santa Monica Bay. Of these, Manhattan Beach *(see p45)* is the most

Yachts in the harbor at Marina del Rey

Hermosa Beach, South Bay

sophisticated, Hermosa (see p45) the liveliest, and Redondo the most historical. A paved trail paralleling the beach and connecting all the three communities is perfect for bicycling and inline skating. ⓢ Map C5

Palos Verdes Peninsula

This posh enclave straddling a rocky precipice is one of the most exclusive in America. A drive along its coastline affords great ocean views with Catalina Island (see pp36–7) in the distance. Malaga Cove and Abalone Cove are popular for tidepool explorations and Point Vicente for whale-watching. Flower lovers should head inland to the sprawling South Coast Botanic Garden. ⓢ Map D6 • Follow Palos Verdes Dr along the coast • Point Vicente Lighthouse, 31501 Palos Verdes Dr West • South Coast Botanic Garden, 26300 Crenshaw Blvd

Wayfarer's Chapel

The most famous structure by Lloyd Wright is a striking 1951 glass and stone memorial to 18th-century theologian Emanuel Swedenborg. The chapel, overlooking the Pacific, is surrounded by landscaped grounds that include a reflecting pool and terraced amphitheater (see p40). ⓢ Map D6 • 5755 Palos Verdes Dr South • 310-377-7919 • Open 8am–5pm • Free

A Day at the Beach

Morning

Start your day with a drive north along the Pacific Coast Highway for glorious ocean views. Travel to sheltered **Paradise Cove** for breakfast at the beachfront restaurant, followed by a couple of hours of frolicking in the surf here or a few miles north at **Zuma Beach** (see p44). Head back south, stopping at **Malibu Adamson House** to admire beautiful ceramic tiles before walking over to **Surfrider Beach** (see p44) to watch the world's finest surfers in action.

Then it's off to **Santa Monica**. Stroll beneath the towering palms of the bluff-top **Palisades Park** (see p43) with the ocean at your feet. For better views of city and sea, treat yourself to a ride on the Ferris wheel on **Santa Monica Pier** and perhaps a snack from one of the many vendors.

Afternoon

For the rest of the afternoon, rent a bicycle and become part of LA's beach scene during an easy ride south to Venice along the paved beachfront bike trail. Park the bike or push it along the bizarre **Venice Boardwalk** (see p122), perhaps stopping to get a tattoo (henna or ink), visit a fortune teller, stock up on unique souvenirs, or tank up on gourmet sausages from **Jodi Maroni's** (see p122). If time permits, continue south to **Marina del Rey**, one of the world's largest yacht harbors, before heading back to Santa Monica where myriad dinner options await.

Around Town – Santa Monica Bay

Following pages **View of Point Vicente Lighthouse in the Palos Verdes Peninsula**

Left **Venice Pier** Center **Muscle Beach Venice** Right **Sidewalk Café**

TOP 10 Venice Boardwalk Attractions

1 Venice Pier
Abbott Kinney built Venice's first pier back in 1905, but the current model dates from 1963. Rescued from demolition in the mid-1980s, the restored fishing pier reopened in 1997.

2 Murals
Numerous murals beautify façades all along the Venice Boardwalk and its side streets. Rip Cronk's *Venice Reconstituted* and *Homage to a Starry Night* are famous. ◈ *Venice Reconstituted, 25 Windward Ave at Speedway • Starry Night, Boardwalk at Wavecrest Ave*

3 Muscle Beach Venice
Check out beefy, hunky bodybuilders with abs of steel at this outdoor gym, successor to the Santa Monica original, which shut in 1959.

4 Basketball Courts
The game's always on at Venice's famous outdoor courts, especially during "Hoops by the Beach," which draws the best street basketball teams.

5 Street Performers
The best in the business, Boardwalk's street performers dance, walk barefoot on glass, balance people on their chin, and even juggle chainsaws.

6 Drum Circle
People of all backgrounds and ages gather on the beach on Sunday afternoons, chanting and dancing to the seductive rhythms of pots, bells, and bottles.

7 Windward Avenue
Flanking Windward Avenue are Venice's oldest Renaissance-style buildings, including St. Marks Hotel, a hostel.

8 Beach Architecture
Unique private homes line the Boardwalk between Venice and Washington Boulevards. Look for the one by Steven Ehrlich at No. 2311 and Frank Gehry's Norton House.

9 Jody Maroni's Sausage Kingdom
The simple sausage goes gourmet at this locally popular but unassuming take-out stand. ◈ *2011 Ocean Front Walk • 310-822-5639*

10 Sidewalk Café
The kitchen produces satisfying sandwiches, salads, and other simple fare. Ideal for people-watching. ◈ *1401 Ocean Front Walk • 310-399-5547*

Homage to a Starry Night mural

The annual "Hoops by the Beach" basketball tournament is held in May every year

Left **Shops lining Main Street** Right **MOCA Store**

ⓉⓄⓅ10 Unique Main Street Boutiques

1 Angel City Books
Bookworms in search of rare and out-of-print books may find what they're looking for. A great café next door. ❧ Map A5 • 218 Pier Ave, just off Main St • 310-399-8767

2 Patagonia
This is the first retail outlet of the maker of innovative outdoor clothing fit for any environment, deserts to the Everest. ❧ Map A5 • 2936 Main St • 310-314-1776

3 The Green Life
This eco-friendly lifestyle shop carries premier green brands and locally made goods, including linens, hair and skin care, toys, and furniture. ❧ Map A5 • 2409 Main St • 310-392-4702

4 Paris 1900
This boudoir-like boutique specializes in lovely romantic antique garments and matching jewelry, accessories, and lacy linens. Even the architecture of the building recalls the joyous frivolity of the Art Nouveau period. ❧ Map A5 • 2703 Main St • 310-396-0405 • Open by appt

5 Arts & Letters
This stationery store stocks hundreds of artist-made greeting cards, pens, and guest books. They also create custom-made invitations. ❧ Map A5 • 2665 Main St • 310-392-9076

6 Le Sanctuaire
A magnet for innovative chefs, this kitchen boutique stocks quality ingredients, over 150 spices and seasonings, cookbooks, equipment, and designer kitchenware. ❧ Map A5 • 2710 Main St • 310-581-8999

7 ZJ Boarding House
This store is for people with a passion for boards – the surf, skate, or snow variety. The knowledgeable staff help to pick through the huge selection of gear and fashion. ❧ Map A5 • 2619 Main St • 800-205-7795

8 Precious Metal Arts
Aspiring jewelers can learn the tricks of the trade during workshops and classes. Glass cases are filled with unique pieces that are for sale. ❧ Map A5 • 2510 Main St • 310-581-4844

9 MOCA Store
A smaller branch of the gift shop at MOCA in Downtown LA (see p72), this is a great place for artsy souvenirs, from posters to jewelry. ❧ Map A5 • 2445 Main St • 310-396-9833

10 Shoop's Delicatessen
This gourmet deli and café stocks Continental delicacies but specializes in hard-to-find German imports. ❧ Map A4 • 2400 Main St • 310-452-1019

Left **Inline Skating** Center **Beach Bike Trail** Right **Surfing**

TOP 10 Outdoor Pursuits

1 Hiking
Around 600 miles (1,000 km) of hiking trails meander through the Santa Monica Mountains, stretching from Griffith Park in Hollywood to the north of Malibu. Will Rogers State Park and Topanga State Park are good gateways for hiking.

2 Inline Skating
Enjoy skating along this 22-mile (35-km) paved trail parallel to the beach from Temescal Canyon Road north of Santa Monica to Torrance Beach. Rental outfitters are abundant in both Santa Monica and Venice.

3 Bicycling
The paved beach path (see above) is equally popular for slow bike cruises. Mountain bikers have plenty of trails to explore in the Santa Monica Mountains.

4 Hang-Gliding
Learn to take to the skies while training on beachside "bunny" hills or launch from a height of 3,500 ft (1,000 m) on a breathtaking flight with an instructor. ✆ Windsports: 818-367-2430, www.windsports.com

5 Sailing
Skipper around the marina or cruise out to the open ocean with your very own sailboat. Rental outfits usually have a variety for you to choose from. ✆ Marina Boat Rentals: Fisherman's Village, Marina del Rey, 310-574-2822

6 Kayaking
One of the nicest places for sea kayaking is off the coast of Catalina Island (see pp36–7). Traveling leisurely by yourself allows you to explore its craggy coastline and to discover your own secret cove.

7 Surfing
The archetypal California watersport is practiced all along the coast – Surfrider Beach (see p44) in Malibu is one of the most famous, but Manhattan Beach (see p45) and Palos Verdes (see p119) are equally popular.

8 Boogie Boarding
Enjoy the thrill of the waves while riding a boogie board to the shore. It's easy and fun. All the towns on the beach have rental stations on or near the sand.

9 Windsurfing
Cabrillo Beach (see p45), nicknamed "Hurricane Gulch," is LA's windsurfing mecca. The harbor side is good for beginners, while advanced surfers can make for the open ocean. ✆ Captain Kirk's (for gear rental & lessons): 310-833-3397

10 Fishing
Fishing without a license is permitted off any ocean pier. Sport fishing boats leave from Fisherman's Village in Marina del Rey (see p118), Shoreline Village in Long Beach, and Ports O' Call Village (see p127) in San Pedro.

Price Categories

Price categories include a three-course meal for one, a glass of house wine, and all unavoidable extra charges including tax.

$	under $25
$$	$25–$50
$$$	$50–$80
$$$$	over $80

Wall murals in Border Grill

🔟 Places to Eat

Inn of the Seventh Ray
Tucked away in leafy Topanga Canyon, this creekside retreat offers organic vegetarian, fish, and chicken dishes seasoned with a generous sprinkling of New Age philosophy. ⊗ Map B3 • 128 Old Topanga Canyon Rd, off Pacific Coast Hwy • 310-455-1311 • $$

Father's Office
This old neighborhood bar has good microbrews and tapas, although regulars swear by the gourmet burger. Delicious fries. ⊗ Map C3 • 1018 Montana Ave, Santa Monica • 310-393-2337 • $

Border Grill
Chefs Mary Sue Milliken and Susan Feniger serve up their unique blend of Mexican flavors. Try the delicious rock shrimp ceviche. ⊗ Map A4 • 1445 4th St, Santa Monica • 310-451-1655 • $$

Jack's on Montana
Located in the ritziest part of Santa Monica, this café features fresh, seasonal, and home-made breads, meats, and veggies. ⊗ Map C3 • 1610 Montana Ave, Santa Monica • 310-453-2771 • $$

Chinois on Main
A Franco-Chinese menu includes Cantonese duck in plum sauce. Jacket and tie required. ⊗ Map C3 • 2709 Main St, Santa Monica • 310-392-9025 • $$$

Joe's Main Street Diner
Joe's has the feel of a neighborhood eatery, but fills up nightly with discerning diners who love Joe Miller's exciting California-French concoctions. ⊗ Map A5 • 1023 Abbott Kinney Blvd, Venice • 310-399-5811 • Closed Mon • $$$

JiRaffe
A local favorite, this romantic spot serves country French and new California cuisine, specializing in fresh, high-quality local ingredients. Outstanding wine list. ⊗ Map A3 • 502 Santa Monica Blvd • 310-917-6671 • Closed Sun • $$$$

Josie
Classic French fare is prepared with organic produce. The Wednesday night Farmers' Market *prix-fixe* menu is top value. ⊗ Map C3 • 2424 Pico Blvd, Santa Monica • 310-581-9888 • $$$$

Uncle Bill's Pancake House
The pancakes and omelets are good, and the tasty French toast, burgers, and salads very popular. ⊗ Map C4 • 1305 Highland Ave, Manhattan Beach • 310-545-5177 • $

Chez Melange
The menu offers a United Nations of dishes, from sushi to kebab and schnitzel. ⊗ Map D5 • 1716 S Pacific Coast Highway, Redondo Beach • 310-540-1222 • $$

Unless otherwise stated, all restaurants accept credit cards, serve vegetarian meals, and provide access for the disabled

125

Left **Shoreline Village** Right **Museum of Latin American Art (MOLAA)**

Long Beach & San Pedro

*S*AN PEDRO AND LONG BEACH *are the maritime muscles fueling LA's reputation as a great trading city. San Pedro supplies much of the manpower that operates the cranes, derricks, tugs, and railway systems in one of the most awesome seaports in the world. Through here pass the goods – automobiles, electronics, and foods – that will make their way to virtually every city in the Americas and Asia. Long Beach, on the other hand, is a city in metamorphosis. Shedding its working-class past, it has become a sophisticated cultural and financial hub. Long Beach's pulse beats strongest along Pine Avenue where indulgences range from Italian Barolo wines to music by Berlioz and belly dance. The grand ocean liner Queen Mary and a defining aquarium are the area's flagship sights.*

Sights

1. Cabrillo Marine Aquarium
2. Los Angeles Maritime Museum
3. Ports O' Call Village
4. Banning Residence Museum
5. Queen Mary
6. Aquarium of the Pacific
7. Museum of Latin American Art (MOLAA)
8. Long Beach Museum of Art
9. Naples & Belmont Shore
10. Ranchos Los Alamitos & Los Cerritos

Canal in residential Naples

Cabrillo Marine Aquarium

Cabrillo Marine Aquarium

Housed in a modern building designed by Frank Gehry, this aquarium *(see p51)* offers plenty to do apart from viewing marine life in its 34 saltwater tanks. Why not try observing newborn jellyfish in the aquatic nursery, listening to whale sounds, or viewing prickly urchins and sea stars in tidepools accessed through the short Cabrillo Coastal Park Trail. ✆ *Map D6 • 3720 Stephen White Drive, San Pedro • 310-548-7562 • Open noon–5pm Tue–Fri, 10am–5pm Sat–Sun • Donation • www.cabrillomarine aquarium.org*

Los Angeles Maritime Museum

This Art Deco museum celebrates LA's seafaring tradition through displays of ship models, photographs, nautical equipment, and memorabilia. A highlight is the exhibit about the USS *Los Angeles*, a navy cruiser that saw battle in China and during the Korean War. A recreated 18-ft (5.4-m) model of the ill-fated *Titanic* is a crowd pleaser. ✆ *Map E6 • Berth 84, at foot of 6th St, San Pedro • 310-548-7618 • Open 10am–5pm Tue–Sun • Adm (free for children) • www.lamaritimemuseum.org*

Figurehead of Queen Victoria in Los Angeles Maritime Museum

Ports O' Call Village

This is a mock New England seaside village geared to catering to tourists. A cobblestone walkway links a variety of shops selling crafts and kitsch. There are also several restaurants, many of them with harbor views. Dine on platters of fresh shrimp, fried calamari rings, and whatever has been freshly caught that morning. For close-up views of supertankers and cargo and cruise ships, join a harbor cruise, which departs from the village. Whale-watching cruises operate from January to March. ✆ *Map E6 • San Pedro waterfront, Berth 77 • 310-548-8076*

Banning Residence Museum

The Greek Revival style home of Phineas Banning (1830–85), the "Father of Los Angeles Harbor," offers a glimpse into the life of one of the most influential of the city's pioneers. Tours take in the office, parlor, family and dining rooms, kitchen, and nursery, all filled with late 19th-century period furniture. ✆ *Map E5 • 401 E M St, Wilmington • 310-548-7777 • Donation • www.banningmuseum.org*

Tours at the Banning Residence Museum start at 12:30pm, 1:30pm, & 2:30pm Tue–Thu & Sat–Sun, & 3:30pm Sat–Sun

Queen Mary

On its maiden voyage in 1936, the *Queen Mary* was the most luxurious liner ever to sail the seven seas. Each crossing carried famous faces, along with thousands of regular vacationers and immigrants. During World War II, she whisked as many as 15,000 soldiers per trip from the USA to Europe. The elegant vessel retired in 1964 and became a tourist attraction three years later. Much of the *Queen Mary*, which also contains a hotel, can be explored on self-guided and guided tours *(see p130)*. ✎ *Map E6 • 1126 Queen Highway, Long Beach • 800-437-2934 • Open 10am–6pm • Adm • www.queenmary.com*

Queen Mary

Aquarium of the Pacific

One of Long Beach's flagship attractions, this high-tech zoo teems with 12,000 fish, birds, and mammals that make their home in the Pacific Ocean. A full-scale model of a blue whale greets visitors in the Great Hall. You'll come face to face with exotic giant spider crabs, playful sea otters, and even get to pet a shark. For a look at what it takes to keep the aquarium afloat, take a Behind-the-Scenes-Tour. ✎ *Map E6 • 100 Aquarium Way, Long Beach • 562-590-3100 • Open 9am–6pm • Closed Dec 25 • Adm • www.aquariumofpacific.org*

Museum of Latin American Art (MOLAA)

Part of Long Beach's emerging East Village Arts District, this lively museum is the only one in the western United States dedicated to showcasing the work of artists who've lived or worked in Latin America since 1945. The collection offers great insight into the culture and concerns of artists from Mexico to Tierra del Fuego and every country in between. The premises have expanded from the original layout and include a sculpture garden. The restaurant on-site is a lovely spot for lunch. ✎ *Map E6 • 628 Alamitos Ave, Long Beach • 562-437-1689 • Open 11am–5pm Wed–Sun (until 9pm Fri) • Adm (free for children under 12) • www.molaa.org*

Long Beach Museum of Art

This small community museum mounts several temporary exhibits annually in addition to showing selections from its permanent collection. On show are paintings and drawings by early 20th-century European and Californian artists along with furniture and decorative objects from throughout American

Log on to www.aquariumofpacific.org for more information on the Aquarium of the Pacific

Cactus Garden in Rancho Los Alamitos

history. The museum enjoys a waterfront location with views of Long Beach's famous offshore oil wells. ✪ Map F6 • 2300 E Ocean Blvd • 562-439-2119 • Open 11am–5pm Fri–Sun (until 8pm Thu) • Adm (free for children under 12) • www.lbma.org

Naples & Belmont Shore
Naples is an Italian-flavored peninsula in Alamitos Bay, which is connected by a causeway to Belmont Shore with its many shopping and dining options. Long Beach's poshest neighborhood, Naples was dreamed up by Arthur Parsons in 1903, around the same time Abbott Kinney conceived of Venice (see p118). Enjoy an authentic Venetian gondola ride (see p138). ✪ Map F6 • Southern Long Beach

Ranchos Los Alamitos & Los Cerritos
In 1784, Manuel Nieto, a corporal in the Spanish army, was granted 300,000 acres of land in recognition of his services. The land was later divided into five ranchos, including Rancho Los Alamitos and Rancho Los Cerritos. The ranch houses are some of the state's oldest structures. ✪ Map F6 • Rancho Los Alamitos, 6400 Bixby Hill Rd, 562-431-3541, Free • Rancho Los Cerritos, 4600 Virginia Rd, 562-570-1755, Free

A Day of Maritime Meandering

Morning

Begin your day at the **Los Angeles Maritime Museum** in San Pedro where you'll find interesting nuggets of information about the city's nautical heritage. A short stroll north through the little park takes you to a modern fire station building at the bottom of 5th Street. It houses a still functional 1925 fire boat capable of pumping over 10,000 gallons (45,000 liters) of water a minute. Historic boat buffs could continue north another half mile (800 m) for a tour of the **SS Lane Victory** at Berth 49, an immaculately restored WWII cargo ship.

Backtrack on foot or take the electric trolley to **Ports O' Call Village** to browse the souvenir shops and have lunch.

Afternoon

Once fortified, join a one-hour narrated cruise for close-ups of the amazing operations of the **Los Angeles Harbor**, the nation's largest.

Head back to your car and drive south on Harbor Boulevard to Pacific Avenue, then left to get to the **Cabrillo Marine Aquarium** for a look at aquatic life in California's waters. For great sunset views, head west on Shepard Street, then north on South Gaffey Street to the bluff-top **Angels Gate Park**. A nice feature here is the Korean Friendship Bell, a replica of an 8th-century original built for a Korean king. Conclude the day with dinner on Pine Avenue in **Long Beach**.

Left **Observation Bar** Right **Wheelhouse**

Features of the Queen Mary

1 Ghost & Legends Tour
This special effects walking tour is hokey and takes you deep into the ship's bowels, including the vast boiler room and the First Class Swimming Pool. ⓢ Adm

2 First Class Swimming Pool
The large lavish pool was once filled with salt water but is empty now and said to be a vortex of ghostly activity.

3 Observation Bar
Visit this Art Deco masterpiece of sparkling chrome and polished hardwood for the carved and curved balustrade and mural painting behind the bar.

4 Engine Room
One of the fastest ocean liners of its time, the *Queen Mary* had a cruising speed of 28.5 knots (34 mph or 55 km/h) and was driven by four steam turbine engines each turning its own propeller.

5 Wheelhouse
Located above the deck officers' quarters, the wheel-house was the navigational control center of the ship. It features dual brass steering wheels and such modern communication equipment as the "loudaphone," an onboard telephone system.

6 Promenade Deck
This deck held most of the First Class common areas as well as the wonderful wooden outdoor walkway, now worn.

7 Queen's Salon
First Class passengers once enjoyed dances, concerts, and religious services in the Promenade Deck grand hall. It is now used for special events.

Detail inside the Queen's Salon

8 Champagne Sunday Brunch
Pick your favorites from 11 culinary stations serving everything from roast beef to salads while a harpist serenades you. It's all set up in the glorious Grand Salon, the original First Class dining room. Reservations are recommended.

9 Sir Winston's
This silver service restaurant was named in honor of the famous British Prime Minister Winston Churchill. During World War II, he traveled to three conferences in the United States aboard the *Queen Mary*.

10 Scorpion
This original Soviet submarine, moored right next to the *Queen Mary*, saw service from 1973 to 1994. A self-guided tour takes in the engine room, the kitchen, and other cramped quarters. ⓢ 10am–6pm • Adm

Price Categories

Price categories include a three-course meal for one, a glass of house wine, and all unavoidable extra charges including tax.

$	under $25
$$	$25–$50
$$$	$50–$80
$$$$	over $80

L'Opera

🔟 Places to Eat

1 L'Opera
A lofty ceiling supported by marble columns provides a wonderfully theatrical setting for tasty fettucine, *frutti di mare*, and *veal scallopine*. ✆ *Map E6 • 101 Pine Ave • 562-491-0066 • $$$*

2 Alegria Cocina Latina
Spanish and Latin American food and a hip crowd make it a popular bistro. Live entertainment on weekends. ✆ *Map E6 • 115 Pine Ave • 562-436-3388 • $$*

3 Veggie Grill
Popular for fresh, tasty dishes that go way beyond the typical vegetarian fare. Options include soy, wheat, nut, and gluten-free dishes. ✆ *Map E6 • 6451 E Pacific Coast Hwy • 562-430-4986 • $*

4 Yard House
This pub crawlers' haunt has almost 200 international brews on tap, from Budweiser to obscure drafts such as Saxer Lemon Lager. ✆ *Map E6 • 401 Shoreline Village Dr • 562-628-0455 • $$*

5 Tequila Jack's
This cantina serves good Mexican food. Try the marvellous tequila straight or blended with a margarita. On Tuesdays, tacos are only a dollar. ✆ *Map E6 • 407 Shoreline Village Dr • 562-628-0454 • $$*

6 The Sky Room
Classic American cuisine and a solid wine list complement the Art Deco style of this restaurant. Live jazz on the weekend draws in the crowds. ✆ *Map F5 • 40 S Locust Ave • 562-983-2703 • $$$*

7 Sir Winston's
Fancy yourself as royalty when dining at this old-fashioned romantic restaurant aboard the *Queen Mary* (see p128). The beef phyllo is recommended. Dress code. ✆ *Map E6 • 1126 Queens Highway • 562-435-3511 • $$$*

8 The Reef
Great views of the Long Beach skyline coupled with delicious fresh fish and seafood. The four-course Sunset Dinner special is a steal. ✆ *Map E6 • 880 Harbor Scenic Dr • 562-435-8013 • $$*

9 Belmont Brewing Co
The tables on the huge deck overlooking the Belmont Pier are the most coveted. Wash down the tasty pizza with the home-made beers. ✆ *Map F6 • 25 39th Place, Belmont Shore • 562-433-3891 • $$*

10 Sushi of Naples
You'll love the sushi and teriyaki chicken. Special combos at lunch and discounted specials at night. ✆ *Map F6 • 5470 E 2nd St, Belmont Shore • 562-434-1122 • $$*

STREETSMART

LOS ANGELES TOP 10

Left **Redondo Beach** Center **Packing right** Right **Distances in miles**

🔟 Planning your Trip

1 When to Go
The chief tourist season in LA is in July and August when the beaches are fairly pleasant, though inland areas can get uncomfortably hot and smoggy. Another good time to visit Los Angeles is in winter, which brings less smog, smaller crowds, and plummeting hotel prices.

2 Weather
LA has a moderate climate with low humidity and cool evenings, even in summer. Rain is most likely from January to March. Summers are sunny and pleasant.

3 What to Pack
Californians dress casually, but LA can be chilly in winter, and even in summer you'll need a jacket or sweater in the evenings, especially near the coast. Sunglasses and hats are must-haves, and are easily-available anywhere in LA.

4 Where to Stay
Los Angeles is huge and offers a wide variety of accomodations. Santa Monica is the most visitor-friendly of the beach towns. Beverly Hills is for the wealthy, while Downtown and Pasadena are great places to stay for culture-vultures and architecture fans. Urban types should opt for the hip and happening Hollywood or West Hollywood.

5 Travel Insurance
Most US insurance is effective throughout the country, but those with foreign insurance coverage should take out comprehensive travel insurance before arriving in the US. Most insurance plans include luggage theft or loss, but what is most crucial is that they should cover medical emergencies.

6 Passports & Visas
Citizens of the UK, Canada, Australia, New Zealand, Ireland, and several other countries need a valid machine-readable passport to visit the US for a period of up to 90 days. US citizens need a passport for re-entry. If you arrive by air or sea, you must present a round-trip ticket. Nationals of some countries must also complete an Electronic System for Travel Authorization (ESTA) application prior to travel. Visit http://travel.state.gov for more details.

7 Electricity
The US has 115-120V current, rather than the 220V current used in other countries. Plugs are of the two-prong variety. Appliances that are not compatible with this electrical system require a transformer and/or an adapter.

8 Measurements
Unlike most other nations, the US does not use the metric system. Weight is measured in ounces, pounds, and tons; distances in inches, feet, yards, and miles; and temperature in Fahrenheit. Carry a pocket converter or conversion chart for convenience.

9 Time
LA is in the Pacific Time Zone, which is eight hours behind GMT – when it's midnight in LA it's 3am the next day in New York, 8am in the UK, 9am in Central Europe, and 6pm in Australia and New Zealand.

10 Children's Needs
If traveling with children, book into child-friendly accommodations – kids can often stay for free in their parents' room (see p149). If you need a baby-sitter, ask the concierge. Most attractions and museums discount admission for children, though age requirements may vary.

Websites

US State Department
www.travel.state.gov/visa

Los Angeles Convention & Visitors Bureau
www.discoverlosangeles.com

Los Angeles Times
www.latimes.com

LA Weekly
www.laweekly.com

Left **Tipping a waiter** Right **LA listings publications**

🔟 General Information

Tipping
In restaurants a tip of 15 to 20 percent is standard. An easy way to figure out the amount is by doubling the sales tax shown on your bill. Cab drivers, masseurs, hairdressers, and other service personnel expect about 10 to 15 percent.

Taxes
The current sales tax in the LA area is 8.25–10.75 percent depending on location. It is added to all restaurant bills and many non-food items, but it is included in gasoline prices, theater tickets, and museum admissions. Services are not taxable. Hotel rooms are subject to a 10–15 percent occupancy tax.

Tourist Offices
LA Inc, the city's visitors bureau, operates two visitor information centers. In addition, cities such as Santa Monica and Beverly Hills have their own offices.

Entertainment Listings
A great source for events listings is the *Los Angeles Times* daily Calendar section; the *LA Weekly*, a freebie available across town, also provides good "what's-on" information.

International Publications
Foreign and out-of-town newspapers and periodicals may be found at the airport, in bookstores such as Barnes & Noble, as well as at specialty newsstands around LA.

Television
All the major TV networks have studios in Los Angeles, including KNBC (Channel 4) and FOX (Channel 11). The smaller WB and UPN networks have merged and are now CW (Channel 5). KCAL (Channel 9) and KCOP (Channel 13) are local stations.

Radio
Numerous radio stations crowd the LA air waves – Jack FM (93.1FM) plays requests, The Wave (94.7FM) offers smooth jazz, KISS (102.7FM) plays Top 40 chart music, and K-Mozart (105.1FM) presents classical sounds. KCRW (89.9F) is LA's main affiliate of NPR (National Public Radio).

Public Holidays
Banks, offices, and some museums are closed on these national holidays – Jan 1, Martin Luther King Jr. Day (3rd Mon in Jan), Presidents' Day (3rd Mon in Feb), Memorial Day (last Mon in May), Independence Day (Jul 4), Labor Day (1st Mon in Sep), Columbus Day (2nd Mon in Oct), Veterans' Day (Nov 11), Thanksgiving (4th Thu in Nov), and Christmas Day (Dec 25).

Opening Hours
Stores in shopping malls and main streets are usually open from 10am to 9pm Monday to Saturday, and to 6pm on Sunday. If you need to cash a traveler's check be aware that most banks are closed on weekends. ATMs, for cash withdrawals, are accessible 24/7.

Discounts
Students, seniors, and children usually qualify for reduced admission at museums and attractions. Proof of age or status may be required.

For information on transportation in LA **See p137**

Left **Los Angeles International Airport (LAX)** Right **LA shuttle**

🔟 Arriving in Los Angeles

Arriving by Air
International and national flights land at Los Angeles International Airport (LAX) and Ontario International Airport (ONT), while smaller airports in Burbank, Irvine, and Long Beach serve only domestic flights.

Customs
Travelers arriving in the US are permitted to import one liter of liquor, 200 cigarettes (or 100 cigars), and $100 worth of gifts ($800 for US or permanent residents) without incurring customs fees. No meat, seeds, plants, or fresh fruit may be brought in.

Immigration
Anyone arriving in the US must complete one customs declaration per household and, in the case of non-citizens, immigration form I-94. Strict security checks, involving the taking of photographs and fingerprints, are now in place for those arriving in the US on a visa.

Los Angeles International Airport (LAX)
LAX occupies a vast plot of land about 5 miles (8 km) south of Santa Monica and 16 miles (25 km) southwest of Downtown and Hollywood. The free Shuttle A bus frequently connects each of the eight terminals, including the Tom Bradley International Terminal.

Shuttles
Several shuttle buses stop outside each terminal on the lower level of LAX. Door-to-door van shuttles are more economical than taxis but take longer. FlyAway runs a service between LAX and Union Station, Irvine, Westwood, and Van Nuys for $5–$25. Most local hotels run a free pick-up service.

Taxis
Taxis must be summoned by a dispatcher waiting outside each terminal on the arrival level. Fares vary but range from $20–35, to Santa Monica, Downtown, and Hollywood. An airport surcharge applies to all trips originating from LAX.

Other LA Area Airports
Domestic travelers might be able to obtain cheaper fares for flights to regional LA airports, which are also smaller and less busy than LAX. Burbank is close to Downtown, Pasadena, and the major movie studios. Airports in Long Beach and Irvine are convenient if you are headed for Disneyland®.

Arriving by Train
Amtrak trains arriving at the historic Union Station in Downtown include the Coast Starlight from Seattle, the Southwest Chief from Chicago, and the Sunset Limited from Orlando. The Pacific Surfliner that travels between San Diego and San Luis Obispo also stops here.

Arriving by Bus
Greyhound operates a vast network of air-conditioned coaches all across the US. Bus travel is cheapest but is much slower and a suitable option only if you're arriving from nearby cities such as San Francisco or Las Vegas. Buses stop at the main Greyhound terminal in an industrial section of Downtown, an area best avoided after dark.

Arriving by Car
Several freeways lead straight to and through LA, including the I-5, Hwy 101, and I-405 from points north; the I-10 from the east; and the I-5 and I-405 from the south.

Note: *Sharp objects such as corkscrews cannot be carried as part of hand luggage while arriving or departing from the US*

Left **LA taxi** Center **Metro Rapid bus** Right **Metro on Red Line**

TOP 10 Getting Around Los Angeles

1 Car Rentals
A car is essential to getting around LA quickly because of the great distances involved. Rentals require a credit card and driver's license. Drivers must be over 21.

2 Rental Insurance
US insurance policies generally cover rental cars as well, while foreign ones almost never do. Check with your insurer for details. Some credit cards may provide secondary coverage if used to pay for the rental.

3 Parking
Free street parking is available in most neighborhoods, although it pays to study the posted restrictions. Stopping or parking is not allowed at red curbs. Some cities, including Santa Monica and Beverly Hills, have inexpensive city-run parking lots. Valet parking is common at restaurants and the better hotels.

4 Driving in LA
LA is relatively easy to navigate. Wearing a seatbelt, even in the backseat, is compulsory. Unless posted otherwise, the speed limit is 35 mph (56 km/h) on city streets and 55 mph (89 km/h) on freeways. Turning right on a red light after stopping at intersections is legal unless otherwise posted. If you use a cell phone while driving, a hands-free set is required.

5 Maps
Locals swear by the book-sized Thomas Guide, but a general street map should suffice for getting around. You'll find these at gas stations or convenience stores, although the most current ones are those published by the American Automobile Association (AAA).

6 Taxis
Getting around town by taxi can be a pricey proposition unless you're traveling as a group or are only going a short distance. Taxi drivers usually won't respond to being hailed but must be ordered in advance.

7 Public Transportation
Getting around LA using public transportation is best reserved for short distances or cross-town travel. The network consists of buses, light rail lines, and a subway line, most of which are run by the Metropolitan Transportation Authority (MTA).

8 Buses
The Downtown DASH buses and the Big Blue Bus in Santa Monica/Venice/Westwood offer good service. For a cheap mini tour, take MTA's express Metro Rapid No. 720 from Santa Monica to Downtown through Beverly Hills, or hop on the Holly Trolley which loops around Hollywood every 12 minutes.

9 Light Rail & Subway
MTA operates three light rail lines – the Blue Line from Downtown to Long Beach, Green Line from Redondo Beach to Norwalk, and Gold Line from Downtown to Pasadena. The Red Line, LA's only subway route, goes from Downtown to Universal City. The Exposition Light Rail line runs from Downtown to Culver City.

10 Walking
Most visitors to LA do as the locals do – they drive. There are some areas that are better for walking in, such as the crowded Downtown or the fun Melrose Avenue and Venice Boardwalk.

Directory

Car Rentals
• Avis: 800-831-2847
• Enterprise: 800-736-8222 • Hertz: 800-654-3131 • National: 800-328-4567

Maps
• AAA: 800-874-7532 (free for members)

Taxis
• Checker: 800-300-5007 • Yellow Cab: 800-200-1085

Public Transportation
• MTA: 800-266-6883

Buses
• Big Blue Bus: 310-451-5444
• DASH: 310-808-2273

Left **Red Line Tours** Center **Cruise tour** Right **The Santa Catalina Island Co. Discovery Tours sign**

🔟 Guided Tours

1 Red Line Tours
During these daily walking tours led by knowledgeable guides, you are made to wear special audio-systems to cut out traffic noise. A great way to learn about Hollywood history, tour the Walk of Fame, or discover the movie star neighborhoods.

2 LA Conservancy Tours
The LA Conservancy conducts wonderful architecture-themed guided walking tours of Downtown every Saturday morning.

3 Segway Tours
Take your pick from the various guided tours on offer, which include the streets and shops of Downtown LA and Beverly Hills, the canals and beaches of Santa Monica and Venice, and the homes of Hollywood stars.

4 Boat Tours
Fisherman's Village in Marina del Rey, San Pedro's Ports O' Call Village, and Shoreline Village in Long Beach are all departure points for various boat cruises, including spins around the harbors and whale-watching trips.

5 Gondola Getaway
Sample the pleasures of the canals of Long Beach's Naples neighborhood aboard an authentic Venetian gondola.

6 Starline Tours
This company offers classic narrated bus tours of LA, including the popular two-hour Movie Stars' Homes Tour and the 5 1/2-hour Grand Tour of Los Angeles. Tours depart throughout the day.

7 Architecture Tours LA
Laura Massino's in-depth tours explore the unique architecture of the city. The tours are organised by area – choices include Hollywood, Silver Lake, Pasadena, and Downtown – and depart daily at 9:30am and 1:30pm.

8 Santa Catalina Island Company Discovery Tours
This company organizes several land- and sea-based excursions lasting from one to four hours. Options include a glass-bottom boat tour and the excellent Island Tour.

9 Art Museum Tours
LACMA in midtown *(see pp16–19)* offers up to five different gallery talks daily. The Getty *(see pp12–15)* also runs daily art, architecture, and garden tours.

10 LA Gang Tours
This tour offers an insight into the gang areas and top crime scene locations in South Central, LA. Each tour bus has a local guide with hands-on experience of the inner city lifestyle.

Directory

Red Line Tours
• Hollywood: 6708 Hollywood Blvd
• Downtown: 304 S Broadway, 323-402-1074

LA Conservancy Tours
• 213-430-4209, www. laconservancy.org

Segway Tours
• Another Side of Los Angeles Tours: 888-878-6079, www.anotherside oflosangelestours.com

Boat Tours
• Hornblower Cruises: 13755 Fiji Way, Marina del Rey, 888-467-6256
• Spirit Cruises: 429 Shoreline Village Dr, 562-435-2668
• Fiesta Harbor Cruise: Ports O'Call Village, Berth 79, San Pedro, 310-831-1906

Gondola Getaway
• 5437 E Ocean Blvd, 562-433-9595, www. gondolagetawayinc.com

Starline Tours
• 800-959-3131, www.starlinetours.com

Architecture Tours LA
• 323-464-7868, www. architecturetoursla.com

Santa Catalina Island Company Discovery Tours
• 800-626-1496

LA Gang Tours
• 213-265-4950, www.lagangtours.com

Rush-hour traffic

🔟 Things to Avoid

1 Rush-hour Traffic
Heavy traffic is one of LA's major drawbacks. To prevent being stuck in a traffic jam, especially on freeways, avoid traveling from 7 to 9am and 4 to 7pm on weekdays. Traffic is also heavy on Sunday afternoons and at the beginning and end of holiday periods.

2 Crime-prone Areas
Visitors to LA rarely fall victim to attacks on person or property. Most areas are perfectly safe for walking around, especially during the day. Keep your wits about you in east LA and south-central LA, and stay away altogether from these neighborhoods after dark. The streets of Hollywood and Venice, and beaches and parks are also dodgy after sundown.

3 Summer Crowds
During the main tourist season in July and August, crowds at major attractions often swell to capacity, especially at big theme parks such as Disneyland® and Universal Studios, where two-hour waits for three-minute rides are common. Remember to pack water and plenty of patience.

4 Ocean Pollution
LA's ocean waters may not be as pristine as those of Polynesia, but they are clean enough for frolicking in the surf at most times. The major exception is after rainy days when garbage flushes straight from the storm drains into the ocean, dangerously raising pollution levels. Swimming is not advised for three days after the rains have stopped.

5 June Gloom
This pesky weather phenomenon arrives almost like clockwork in late spring, cloaking the entire city in a thick layer of fog and clouds that last days and weeks at a time. However, the fog usually burns off by late afternoon.

6 Sightseeing Excesses
LA novice visitors sometimes make the mistake of packing too much sightseeing into a single day, which can be exhausting. Don't underestimate the time it takes to travel between attractions or the tiring summer heat. If limited time is a factor, join an organized tour or focus your explorations on a single neighborhood.

7 Traveling during Major Holidays
Higher costs, packed planes and airports, frayed nerves, and crowded attractions are among the main factors that make travel during major holidays *(see p135)* a stressful affair. Avoid scheduling your trip around Easter, Memorial Day, July 4, Labor Day, Thanksgiving, Christmas, and New Year's Day.

8 Road Rage
As if LA's heavy traffic wasn't bad enough, many people tend to adopt an unpleasant and aggressive attitude behind the wheel. Sudden lane changes right in front of you, not allowing you to change lanes, or driving right behind you are just some of the antics. Keep your cool and don't allow the situation to escalate. In case the situation worsens, make sure your car doors are locked.

9 Going Topless
Compared to most European nations, America is, overall, a rather prudish country. Dropping your bikini top on the beach will not only generate unwelcome stares but quite possibly, a fine as well. Most restaurants, even casual ones located on the beach, require a minimum of shorts, a t-shirt, and shoes.

10 Public Drinking
Drinking on the sidewalk, the beach, in a park, or any other public space is prohibited by law, and you will be fined if caught. It is also illegal to have an open container of alcohol in your car.

Left **Go Los Angeles Card** Center **A hostel sign** Right **Flea market at Melrose Trading Post**

🔟 Los Angeles on a Budget

1 Free Sightseeing
Some of the best things to do in Los Angeles don't cost a cent – go to the beach, stroll down the Venice Board-walk, hike up the Santa Monica Mountains, tour the Getty Center, or listen to street musicians on the Third Street Promenade.

2 Museums
Some of LA's finest museums, including the Getty Center, the California Science Center, and the California African American Museum, do not charge admission. Many others are free one day a week or once a month *(see individual listings in this book for more details).*

3 Go Los Angeles Card & City Pass Hollywood
If you're planning to immerse yourself in Hollywood glamour there are two types of passes that allow admission to several sights for a nominal sum. The Go Los Angeles Card offers 1- to 7-day passes and gives you access to more than 40 attractions, museums, and tours. The City Pass Hollywood buys admis-sion to five attractions over a 14-day period. Visit www.smartdestinations.com and www.citypass.com for details.

4 Free Events
Summer is a great time for free outdoor concerts and events.

Venues hosting regular performances include the Santa Monica Pier, the Getty Center, the Skirball Center, and the Water Court near MOCA. Free festivals celebrating LA's multicultural tapestry take place all year.

5 Free TV Shows
Watch your favorite TV stars in action by attending a live taping at a major studio. Free tick-ets are available through Audiences Unlimited or from studio audience scouts in places such as the Venice Boardwalk or the Farmers Markets.

6 Lodging
While hostels are great for gregarious types, chain motels are best for budget travelers in need of privacy. Some motels and hotels offer American Automobile Association members a discount. Bar-gaining is possible during the slack tourist season. Look for coupon maga-zines available at restau-rants and tourist offices.

7 Shopping
Bargains abound in LA, with department stores and boutiques mounting special sales year-round, especially around public holidays. For extra savings, look for coupons in the Sunday *Los Angeles Times.* Flea markets, vintage stores, and thrift shops offer unique finds at cut-throat prices.

8 Restaurants
Filling up for little money is easy in LA. Fast-food and chain restaurants are ubiquitous, of course, but it's also possible to eat cheaply at better res-taurants. Go for lunch instead of dinner, avoid ordering alcoholic drinks, and take advantage of promotions or "early bird" specials served before the dinner rush.

9 Happy Hours
During happy hours, bars and restaurants offer discounted drinks and free snacks or special-value appetizer meals. Happy hours are usually held between 5pm and 7pm on weekdays, but hours and days vary according to each establishment.

10 Theater Tickets
There's plenty of live theater in LA, but tickets can be expensive. Half-price tickets for selected plays are available on the Internet through the popular Theatre In LA.

Directory

Free Events
• *City of Los Angeles Cultural Affairs Dept:* 213-202-5500, www.culturela.org

Free TV Shows
• *Audiences Unlimited:* 818-753-3470, www.tvtickets.com

Theater Tickets
• *Theatre In LA:* www.theatreinla.com

Left **Automated Teller Machine (ATM)** Center **Phone card** Right **US Mail van**

🔟 Banking & Communications

Streetsmart

Banking Hours
Most banks are open from Monday through Friday, usually from 9am or 10am to 6pm; a few branches also do business on Saturday until 1pm or 2pm. Branches of Wells Fargo, Bank of America, and Chase can be found all across LA.

ATMs
Automated Teller Machines (ATMs) are found at almost all banks and are open 24 hours a day. Most are equipped to handle transactions using bank and credit cards linked to one of the worldwide networks, such as Star, Plus, or Cirrus. A small fee is usually required.

Credit Cards
A credit card is a very common form of payment in the US, with nearly universal acceptance of MasterCard and Visa and, to a lesser extent, American Express. Cash advances from ATMs using credit cards mostly start accruing interest immediately.

Traveler's Checks
Traveler's checks in US dollars are widely accepted in restaurants, supermarkets, banks, and stores; personal checks on an out-of-state or foreign account are not. Practically all banks cash traveler's checks for a fee; American Express offices cash their company-issued checks for free. Bring a passport or some form of government-issued photo ID.

Public Pay Phones
Public telephones have all but disappeared from the streets of LA, but you may still be able to find them in airports, some libraries, restaurants, and at well-used beaches. Many phones only accept coins. A better option for visitors is to buy a disposable cell phone with pre-paid minutes from a convenience or electronics store.

Phone Cards
Prepaid phone cards eliminate the need for coins at pay phones and may also help save on calls placed from hotels. Available in many supermarkets, gas stations, and electronics stores in amounts starting at $5, they require you to dial a toll-free access number before making your call. Read the small print as some of the less respectable ones come with extra charges on top of the per minute rate.

Post Office Hours
General post office hours are 8am to 5pm Monday to Friday and 8am to 2pm Saturday, though timings may vary slightly from branch to branch. Many larger post offices offer 24-hour Automated Postal Centers (APCs), self-service kiosks where you can buy stamps and ship packages. For specifics and branch locations, call 800-275-8777. Stamps are available in supermarkets and some ATMs.

Sending Mail
Visit www.usps.com for an up-to-date breakdown of postal rates.

Express & Courier Mail
The US Postal Service (USPS) offers overnight service within the US, and global two- to three-day delivery. FedEx and UPS are the dominant private courier services.

Internet Access
Many hotels have free data port connections for laptop Internet access. In addition, several hotels offer free Wi-Fi Internet access in the lobby and in the rooms. Free Wi-Fi is also available in many of the city's libraries and coffee shops.

Directory

Express & Courier Mail
• USPS:
800-222-1811
• FedEx:
800-247-4747
• UPS:
800-742-5877

Wi-Fi FreeSpot Directory
• www.wififreespot.com

Left **Ambulance** Center **Sign for a 24-hour pharmacy** Right **Pharmacy store**

TOP 10 Security & Health

1 Emergency Numbers
Dial 911 for any kind of emergency (ambulance, police, fire, etc). A toll-free number, it will be answered by an operator who will send out the respective emergency response service.

2 Medical Assistance
In a serious emergency, medical assistance is available 24 hours a day in hospital emergency rooms. Cheaper alternatives are urgent care clinics, which accept patients on a walk-in basis. Call your insurance company for a referral to a local doctor or check the Yellow Pages in case of non-emergencies.

3 Free & Low-cost Clinics
If traveling without insurance, you can keep medical costs low by visiting a subsidized clinic.

4 Pharmacies
Major drugstore chains such as CVS, Longs Drugs, and Rite Aid contain full-service pharmacies, most of which keep late hours (many remain open 24 hours a day). If you take prescription drugs, it's best to bring along your own supply.

5 Health Insurance
Most US policies are effective throughout the country, but those with foreign insurance coverage should take out medical insurance before arriving in the US, where healthcare costs tend to be astronomical.

6 Sun Protection
Lathering up with sunscreen is essential in the fierce California sunshine unless you want to walk around with the complexion of a boiled lobster. Remember that UVA and UVB rays can do their damage even in cloudy weather.

7 Water Quality
LA tap water is heavily chlorinated and not particularly tasty despite being perfectly drinkable. Most people prefer bottled water, which is widely available. Free water served in restaurants is always tap water. The water quality in Santa Monica Bay has improved significantly in the last decade, making swimming in the ocean safe in most places, except after rainstorms when pollution levels rise temporarily (see p139).

8 Smoking
Lighting up is illegal in most public places, including airports, post offices, stores, theaters, as well as in all restaurants and cafés, though some allow smoking at outdoor tables. Some bars and nightclubs have separate outdoor areas for smoking.

9 Safety
Despite a reputation to the contrary, Los Angeles is a fairly safe city, especially in neighborhoods with the greatest appeal for tourists. Of course, common sense applies – be aware of your surroundings when using the ATM, watch your purse or wallet in crowded areas, and remember to lock your hotel room before leaving (see p139).

10 Theft
Having personal property stolen is the most likely crime you might encounter in LA. As a general rule, be wary of pickpockets in crowded areas, keep valuables locked in the hotel safe or carry them close to your body, and remember not to leave items visible in your car.

Directory

Emergency Numbers
• Travelers Aid: 310-646-2270 • Crisis Hotline: 310-392-8381

Free & Low-cost Clinics
• Venice Family Clinic: 604 Rose Ave, 310-392-8636 • Saban Free Clinic: 6043 Hollywood Blvd, 8405 Beverly Blvd, 5205 Melrose Ave

Pharmacies
• 24-hour Pharmacy: 888-443-5701

Left **Disabled parking sign** Center **Ramp for wheelchair** Right **Traveling with children**

TOP 10 Special Concerns

1 Disabled Travelers
Los Angeles is a relatively accessible town for those with visual, mobility, or hearing impairments. Most public buildings, museums, and restaurants have ramps and special bathrooms for the wheelchair-bound. Curbs are cut to facilitate movement, hotels have rooms with extra wide doors, and car rental agencies offer special hand-controlled cars.

2 Public Transportation for the Disabled
Nearly all buses and railway cars operated by MTA, LA's main public transportation agency, are accessible to people in wheelchairs. Buses are equipped with wheelchair lifts and all Metro Rail stations have walkways, ramps, or elevators. Metro's Access Services Incorporated also provides transportation for disabled people.

3 Senior Citizens
Almost all museums and attractions in Los Angeles offer discounted admission to senior citizens, though age limits at which these kick in range from 50 to 65. Airlines, Amtrak trains, and Greyhound buses may also offer reduced rates. Members of the American Association of Retired Persons (AARP) qualify for certain additional benefits.

4 Women Travelers
LA is a cosmopolitan city, and women travelers should not have any special problems. Gaining admission to trendy nightclubs is much easier for women than for men.

5 Gay & Lesbian Travelers
LA has a large gay and lesbian community, which is centered in West Hollywood; Santa Monica Boulevard, especially, is packed with happening bars, restaurants, and fitness clubs.

6 Resources for Gays & Lesbians
The LA Gay and Lesbian Center is the main local advocacy group, which also offers counseling and confidential AIDS tests. Free magazines are available in bars, eateries, and bookshops.

7 Student Travelers
LA doesn't have a dedicated "Latin Quarter," though Westwood Village, next to UCLA, probably comes closest. Most of the beach towns have serious party scenes, especially Venice and Hermosa Beach. STA Travel, a student-oriented travel agency, has several branches in town.

8 Tips for Student Travelers
Always carry your student ID to qualify for a range of discounts, from transportation to movie tickets. Foreign students should carry an International Student Identity Card (ISIC). The legal drinking age in the US is 21.

9 Traveling with Children
Shopping malls, public restrooms, restaurants, and departmental stores have diaper-changing stations. Most restaurants have highchairs.

10 Dietary Concerns
Vegetarians, vegans, weight-watchers, or anybody else in need of a special diet will be well catered to in LA. Even if restaurant menus don't feature the required, chefs usually accommodate most preferences.

Directory

Public Transportation for the Disabled
• MTA emergency hotline: 800-621-7828
• Access Services Inc: 800-827-0829

Senior Citizens
• AARP: 888-687-2277, www.aarp.org

Resources for Gays & Lesbians
• LA Gay & Lesbian Center: 1625 N Schrader Blvd, 323-993-7400, www.lagaycenter.org

Student Travelers
• STA Travel: 920 Westwood Blvd, 310-824-1574

Left **The Four Seasons** Center **Beverly Wilshire** Right **Terranea Resort**

🔟 Bastions of Luxury

1 Terranea Resort
Located on the Palos Verdes Peninsula, with splendid views over the ocean and Catalina Island, this eco-friendly resort boasts 400 rooms, suites, and bungalows. Guests can while away the time at the luxury spa, with 24 treatment rooms, at the nine-hole golf course, or enjoying the gastronomic offerings of the restaurant. ◈ Map D6 • 6610 Palos Verdes Dr S • 310-273-2433 • $$$$
• www.terranea.com

2 The Four Seasons
Enormous floral arrangements welcome guests to this refined hotel whose delights include a full-service spa and free limousine rides within a 2-mile (3-km) radius. At the Windows Lounge you may find yourself sipping cocktails next to someone famous. Children under 18 stay free with parents. ◈ Map K5 • 300 S Doheny Dr • 310-273-2222 • $$$$$
• www.fourseasons.com

3 Beverly Wilshire
Overlooking Rodeo Drive, this dignified 1928 hotel has hosted royalty many times and featured prominently in the 1990 movie Pretty Woman. Luxurious extras include chauffeured car service within a radius of 3 miles (5 km). ◈ Map C2 • 9500 Wilshire Blvd • 310-275-5200 • $$$$$ • www. fourseasons.com

4 Ritz-Carlton Los Angeles
This sleek, modern, highly luxurious hotel is close to Staples, the Nokia Theatre, and top shopping and dining. It shares a tower with the Marriott at LA LIVE and has a posh rooftop pool and bar on the 26th floor. ◈ Map S6 • 900 W Olympic Blvd • 213-743-8800 • $$$$$
• www.ritzcarlton.com

5 The Peninsula Beverly Hills
Antiques and artwork grace rooms, suites, and villas, all brimming with high-tech features, including wireless web access and satellite TV. A personal room valet attends to your every need. ◈ Map C2 • 9882 S Santa Monica Blvd • 310-551-2888 • $$$$$
• www.peninsula.com

6 L'Ermitage Beverly Hills
Discretion is key at this sophisticated Beverly Hills hideaway with the full range of in-room high-tech amenities. Enjoy panoramic views from the rooftop pool flanked by cabanas for extra privacy. Even pets get the royal treatment. ◈ Map K5 • 9291 Burton Way • 310-278-3344 • $$$$$
• www.viceroyhotelsand resorts.com/beverlyhills

7 Hotel Oceana
One of Santa Monica's prettiest hotels, the Oceana has flirtatiously colorful decor, reminiscent of the French Riviera. Many of the large suites have views of the ocean. ◈ Map C3 • 849 Ocean Ave • 310-393-0486 • $$$$$ • www.hotel oceanasantamonica.com

8 The Fairmont Miramar
On the site of the private home of Santa Monica's founder, Senator John Jones, the Miramar has welcomed guests since the roaring 1920s. For the ultimate in luxury, book a poolside garden bungalow. ◈ Map A3 • 101 Wilshire Blvd • 310-576-7777 • $$$$
• www.fairmont.com

9 Shutters on the Beach
This delightful hotel right by the sands of Santa Monica takes the beach cottage to new heights. Relax on fluffy mattresses, feel the cool ocean breeze, or watch the warm California sunlight filtering in through the shutters. ◈ Map A4 • 1 Pico Blvd • 310-458-0030 • $$$$$ • www. shuttersonthebeach.com

10 Casa del Mar
An imposing presence overlooking Santa Monica Beach, this 1926 beach club has been restored to its original grandeur. The grand, lavish lobby sets the tone for cosily decorated rooms. ◈ Map A4 • 1910 Ocean Way • 310-581-5533 • $$$$$
• www.hotelcasadelmar.com

Unless otherwise stated, all hotels accept credit cards, have private bathrooms and air conditioning, and provide disabled access

Price Categories

For the cheapest standard double room per night (without breakfast), taxes, and extra charges.

$	under $100
$$	$100–$150
$$$	$150–$250
$$$$	$250–$350
$$$$$	over $350

Casa Malibu Inn

TOP 10 Beach Hotels

1 Malibu Beach Inn
Enjoy spectacular views of the coastline from Malibu's only luxury beachfront hotel with a red-tiled Mission-style building. All rooms have gas fireplaces and balconies, some with Jacuzzis. A free Continental breakfast buffet is served. ® *Map A3 • 22878 Pacific Coast Hwy • 310-456-6444 • $$$$ • www.malibubeachinn.com*

2 Casa Malibu Inn
This Mediterranean-style charmer is located on one of the most beautiful stretches of the California coast. Hit the waves from the private beach of the Casa Malibu Inn, then enjoy a delicious Continental breakfast. Some rooms have a kitchen and a cosy fireplace. ® *Map A3 • 22752 Pacific Coast Hwy • 310-456-2219 • No dis. access • $$$*

3 JW Marriott Santa Monica Le Merigot
Centrally located, this Santa Monica hotel has the elegant personality of a Mediterranean mansion. Rooms are dressed in sunny, golden colors and feature patios, heavenly beds, and big desks. Bold chandeliers light up the Cézanne restaurant, where you can taste exquisite French cuisine. Excellent in-house spa. ® *Map A4 • 1740 Ocean Ave • 310-395-9700 • $$$$$ • www.marriott.com*

4 Hotel California
This delightful Santa Monica cottage trades grandness for whimsy. Blonde wood furniture, hardwood floors, and hand-painted surfboards doubling as headboards add to the breezy feel. ® *Map B3 • 1670 Ocean Ave • 310-393-2363 • Dis. access in one suite • No air conditioning • $$$ • www.hotelca.com*

5 Cadillac Hotel
Charlie Chaplin liked to spend summers in this pink and turquoise Art Deco landmark on Venice Boardwalk. Clean but basic rooms, including some four-bed dorms. ® *Map A5 • 8 Dudley Ave • 310-399-8876 • No air conditioning • $ • www.thecadillachotel.com*

6 Hotel Erwin
This boutique beach hotel is located close to Venice Beach and Santa Monica Pier and gives you easy access to interesting cafés and stores. Its 119 guestrooms come with the full range of amenities. The hotel has a fitness suite and rates include Continental breakfast. ® *Map A6 • 1697 Pacific Ave • 310-452-1111 • Dis. access in two rooms • $$$ • www.hotelerwin.com*

7 Jamaica Bay Inn
For beachfront on a budget, opt for this pleasant Marina del Rey hotel right on Mother's Beach. The sand-colored rooms have private patios or balconies. ® *Map C3 • 4175 Admiralty Way • 310-823-5333 • No dis. access • $$$ • www.jamaicabayinn.com*

8 Ritz-Carlton Marina del Rey
Overlooking the world's largest custom-built pleasure boat harbor, the Ritz-Carlton offers European elegance and deluxe creature comforts. Indulge in global cuisine at the stylish Jer-ne restaurant. ® *Map C3 • 4375 Admiralty Way • 310-823-1700 • $$$$$ • www.ritzcarlton.com*

9 Beach House at Hermosa Beach
Within earshot of the waves, this casually elegant getaway is the perfect antidote to stress. Just relax in front of the crackling fire in your roomy suites. ® *Map C5 • 1300 The Strand • 310-374-3001 • $$$$ • www.beach-house.com/hermosa-beach*

10 Sea Sprite Motel & Apartments
Rooms in this Hermosa Beach hotel won't win the style awards, but with a location right on the beach, you probably won't spend much time inside. Larger units sleep up to six. ® *Map C5 • 1016 The Strand • 310-376-6933 • No dis. access • No air conditioning • $$$ • www.seaspritemotel.com*

Left **Langham Huntington Hotel** Center **Chateau Marmont** Right **Hotel Queen Mary**

Historic Charmers

Figueroa Hotel
This hotel's unique personality greets you as soon as you enter its soaring columned lobby with colorful tiles and exotic furnishings. The rooms offer basic comforts and a lovely color-splashed Moroccan theme. ✆ *Map T5 • 939 S Figueroa St • 213-627-8971 • $$ • www.figueroahotel.com*

Langham Huntington Hotel
A grand old-world style resort, this is a destination in itself. Have your breakfast alfresco and lounge by the Olympic-sized pool, followed by a pampering session in the full-service spa. Enjoy high tea in the afternoon, then hit the tennis courts before changing for dinner at the elegant restaurant. A perfect day, indeed! ✆ *Map F2 • 1401 S Oak Knoll Ave • 626-568-3900 • $$$$ • www.pasadena.langhamhotels.com*

Hollywood Roosevelt
A stone's throw away from Hollywood and Highland is this famous Hollywood hotel. While the grand lobby pays homage to the original Spanish-Mediterranean decor, most rooms have 21st-century amenities. Only the poolside cabanas retain an old-fashioned flair. ✆ *Map P2 • 7000 Hollywood Blvd • 323-466-7000 • $$$$ • www.thompsonhotels.com*

Chateau Marmont
Famous recluses such as Greta Garbo holed up in this quirky French castle-style hotel, whose policy of discretion still ensures steady celebrity bookings. Revel in Hollywood lore in the cottages, bungalows, and suites. ✆ *Map M3 • 8221 W Sunset Blvd • 323-656-1010 • $$$$ • www.chateaumarmont.com*

Sunset Tower Hotel
Once the home of John Wayne and mobster Bugsy Siegel, the Sunset Tower is a striking 1929 Art Deco tower. The former apartments are now luxuriously appointed rooms and suites, with reproductions of 1920s period furniture. ✆ *Map M3 • 8358 Sunset Blvd • 323-654-7100 • $$$$ • www.sunsettowerhotel.com*

The Georgian Hotel
This 1933 seaside hotel was an instant hit with the movie elite seeking to escape the Hollywood heat. Behind the Art Deco façade await guest rooms in chocolate colors, most with ocean views. ✆ *Map A4 • 1415 Ocean Ave • 310-395-9945 • $$$ • www.georgianhotel.com*

Beverly Hills Hotel
It's no longer the trendiest of LA's luxury hotels, but its exalted place in Hollywood history remains. Drinks in the Polo Lounge, tanning by the poolside, and opulent comforts are all part of the unforgettable experience. ✆ *Map J4 • 9641 Sunset Blvd • 310-276-2251 • $$$$$ • www.beverlyhillshotel.com*

Shangri-la Hotel
Dating from 1939, this hotel doesn't quite manage to combine nostalgia with modern amenities. However, its oceanfront Santa Monica location is great and the large rooms have ocean views. Rates include parking, a small breakfast, and tea. ✆ *Map A3 • 1301 Ocean Ave • 310-394-2791 • $$$ • www.shangrila-hotel.com*

Hotel Queen Mary
Stay in the roomy quarters of the *Queen Mary* with their polished wood and thick carpets to savor the romantic ambience of a bygone era *(see p128 & p130)*. ✆ *Map E6 • 1126 Queens Hwy • 562-435-3511 • $$$ • www.queenmary.com*

Zane Grey Pueblo Hotel
Built by American Western writer Zane Gray in 1926, this is a charming rustic retreat on Catalina Island with lovely views of the yacht-dotted Avalon Bay. An excellent getaway from the bustle of big city LA. ✆ *199 Chimes Tower Rd, Avalon • 310-510-0966 • No dis. access • No air conditioning • $$ • www.zanegreypueblohotel.com*

Unless otherwise stated, all hotels accept credit cards, have private bathrooms and air conditioning, and provide disabled access

Price Categories

For the cheapest standard double room per night (without breakfast), taxes, and extra charges.

$	under $100
$$	$100–$150
$$$	$150–$250
$$$$	$250–$350
$$$$$	over $350

Left **Mondrian** Right **Maison 140**

Chic & Hip Hotels

1 The Standard Downtown

Downtown's first trendy hotel made an immediate splash when it debuted in 2002. The rooftop bar with its balmy pool and trendy scene is the place to be. Rooms are large with minimalist interiors. ® Map U4 • 550 S Flower St • 213-892-8080 • $$$ • www.standardhotels.com

2 Mondrian

The rooms seem an afterthought at New York hotelier Ian Schrager's celebrity outpost. The Cuban-Asian eatery, pool deck, and hip Sky Bar provide stylish hobnobbing territory. ® Map M3 • 8440 Sunset Blvd • 323-650-8999 • $$$$$ • www.mondrianhotel.com

3 The Standard Hollywood

Shag is back and the pool is cool at this good-value retro hangout on Sunset Strip. Party in the lobby, which morphs into a lounge at night with DJ-spun music. The pool, intriguingly fringed by indigo-blue Astroturf, is also good for loitering. ® Map M3 • 8300 Sunset Blvd • 323-650-9090 • $$$ • www.standardhotels.com

4 The Grafton on Sunset

Standing next to the Mondrian, the Grafton has a more accessible and low-key ambience. The lobby is flanked by the fashionable Balboa Lounge and a steakhouse and leads to the pool. ® Map L3 • 8462 W Sunset Blvd • 323-654-4600 • $$$ • www.graftononsunset.com

5 Sunset Marquis Hotel & Villas

This ultra-deluxe West Hollywood hideaway is a favorite with rock'n'roll royalty such as U2. The on-site recording studio is a major draw, but so are the luxurious quarters and the Bar 1200 Cocktail Lab (see p61 & p65). ® Map L3 • 1200 N Alta Loma Rd • 310-657-1333 • $$$$$ • www.sunsetmarquis.com

6 Elan Hotel

The lobby and lounge at this stylish boutique hotel display the retro-cool look in vogue, while the rooms are done up in calming natural tones. It's close to some of the city's finest attractions, and you could also order room service and pick a movie from the video library. ® Map L5 • 8435 Beverly Blvd • 866-203-2212 • Disabled access in one room • $$$ • www.elanhotel.com

7 Maison 140

An intimate B&B in the former villa of silent movie star Lillian Gish, Maison 140 cleverly fuses French and Asian design accents. Every room is different, but all feature patterned wallpaper and European antiques. The seductively lit Bar Noir is great for a nightcap.

Excellent value for money, close to Rodeo Drive. ® Map J6 • 140 Lasky Dr • 310-281-4000 • $$$$ • www.maison140.com

8 Avalon

This cool Beverly Hills hot spot has intimately lit cabanas that fringe the curvaceous pool. Rooms feature George Nelson lamps and Eames-style chairs. And don't forget – Marilyn Monroe once lived here. ® Map K6 • 9400 W Olympic Blvd • 310-277-5221 • $$$$ • www.viceroyhotelgroup.com/avalon

9 W Los Angeles

The chic W is full of surprises, such as the "waterfall" entrance steps and the table games in the lobby. Suites are fully wired for connectivity, and the Mojo eatery and lobby bar are weekend hot spots. ® Map C2 • 930 Hilgard Ave • 310-208-8765 • $$$$ • www.wlosangeles.com

10 Viceroy

The couple behind the stylish Maison 140 and Avalon has created a fantasy environment that transports guests back in time to Colonial England. The decor mixes kitsch and sophistication, with a grown-up color palette of grey, bright green, and soothing cream. ® Map A4 • 1819 Ocean Ave • 310-260-7500 • $$$$$ • www.viceroyhotelsandresorts.com/santamonica

Room rates may vary with season, availability, and specials and promotions; all prices listed are high-season rates

Left & Right **Hollywood Celebrity Hotel**

TOP 10 Budget Hotels & Hostels

1 Stillwell Hotel
One of the best bargains in Downtown, the Stillwell puts you within walking distance of the Staples Center. It's in a well restored early 20th-century building and has a popular Indian restaurant and a graceful old-time cocktail lounge. ✎ Map T5 • 838 S Grand Ave • 213-627-1151 • $ • www.stillwell-hotel.com

2 Hollywood Celebrity Hotel
Despite the name, celebrity encounters are exceedingly unlikely in this budget gem, a stone's throw away from Hollywood and Highland. But the inviting burgundy awning and Art Deco lobby lead to nicely sized rooms with walls with cartoonlike murals. Rates include a small breakfast as well as parking. ✎ Map P2 • 1775 Orchid Ave • 323-850-6464 • $$ • www.hotelcelebrity.com

3 Hollywood Orchid Suites Hotel
An excellent base of operation for those wanting plenty of space. Some suites are like small apartments with full kitchen, living room, and bedroom. The decor is a bit long in the tooth, but it's all well kept. With a pool and rooftop sundeck for perks, this place offers good value, indeed. ✎ Map P2 • 1753 Orchid Ave • 323-874-9678 • $$ • www.orchidsuites.com

4 USA Hostel
Those traveling on a tight budget will find this friendly Hollywood hostel a good jumping-off place for their explorations. Rates include hot beverages, pancake breakfast, linen, and lockers. The lounge has a view of the Hollywood Sign. ✎ Map Q2 • 1624 Schrader Blvd • 323-462-3777 • $ • www.usahostels.com

5 Beverly Laurel Motor Hotel
This 1950s-style motel with a small pool is within walking distance of the Farmers Market, Melrose Avenue, and the Beverly Center. Framed art and cheerful bedspreads adorn the rooms. The downstairs diner, Swingers, is popular (see p109). ✎ Map M4 • 8018 Beverly Blvd • 323-651-2441 • No dis. access • $

6 Highland Gardens Hotel
A large pool and tropical garden give this hotel near the Walk of Fame an old-Hollywood atmosphere. Rooms are basic, with fridges and Wi-Fi. Rates include parking and Continental breakfast. ✎ Map P2 • 7047 Franklin Ave • 323-850-0536 • $$ • www.highlandgardenshotel.com

7 Farmer's Daughter Hotel
The "price is right" at this motel opposite the Original Farmers Market and CBS, which explains its popularity with game show contestants taping at the TV studio. The staff is willing to organize tickets if you'd like to be part of the audience. ✎ Map M5 • 115 S Fairfax Ave • 800-334-1658 • $ • www.farmersdaughterhotel.com

8 Sea Shore Motel
A Santa Monica budget abode, it is perfect for those who favor location over luxury. Only two blocks from the beach, it is on trendy Main Street with wonderful shopping and dining. ✎ Map A5 • 2637 Main St • 310-392-2787 • $ • www.seashoremotel.com

9 Inn at Venice Beach
The beach beckons outside this small hotel on the border of Venice and Marina del Rey. Rooms offer moderate comforts and a cheerful decor. Rates include breakfast. ✎ Map A6 • 327 Washington Blvd • 310-821-2557 • No dis. access • $$$ • www.innatvenicebeach.com

10 Safari Inn
Easily recognized by its classic neon sign, this retro motel has undergone a facelift. Rooms, some with full kitchens, now sparkle in peach and blue. Close to Universal, NBC, and Warner Bros Studios. ✎ Map E3 • 1911 W Olive Ave • 818-845-8586 • $$ • www.coasthotels.com

Unless otherwise stated, all hotels accept credit cards, have private bathrooms and air conditioning, and provide disabled access

Price Categories

For the cheapest standard double room per night (without breakfast), taxes, and extra charges.

$	under $100
$$	$100–$150
$$$	$150–$250
$$$$	$250–$350
$$$$$	$over $350

Loews Santa Monica Beach Hotel

🔟 Family Hotels & Motels

1 Beverly Garland's Holiday Inn

Conveniently located close to Universal Studios. Special children's suites with bunk beds and play stations are available and breakfast is free for under 12s. Facilities include pool and tennis courts. ✆ Map D1 • 4222 Vineland Ave, North Hollywood • 818-238-3759 • $$ • www.beverlygarland.com

2 Magic Castle Hotel

Pennywise travelers love this hotel close to Hollywood action. Units vary in size but full kitchens help cut down on restaurant bills. Guests also enjoy access privileges to the Magic Club in a nearby mansion. ✆ Map P2 • 7025 Franklin Ave • 800-741-4915 • No dis. access • $$$ • www.magiccastlehotel.com

3 Best Western Hollywood Hills

Other hotels may have more stylish rooms, but the ones at this central Hollywood property offer plenty of elbow space. The tiled pool and coffee shop are welcome assets. ✆ Map Q2 • 6141 Franklin Ave • 323-464-5181 • $$ • www.bestwestern.com

4 Sheraton Universal Hotel

Although this property can't shake off the institutional feel of a chain hotel, its location next to Universal Studios is a bonus. Free shuttles to Universal. ✆ Map D2 • 333 Universal Hollywood Dr • 818-980-1212 • $$$ • www.starwoodhotels.com

5 Hotel Palomar Los Angeles

Located in Westwood village, this family hotel allows you easy access to lots of shops, restaurants, and theaters. It includes a full-service restaurant, bar, swimming pool, gym, and gift shop. ✆ Map C2 • 10740 Wilshire Blvd • 310-475-8711 • $$$ • www.hotelpalomar-lawestwood.com

6 Hotel Beverly Terrace

Walking distance from Rodeo Drive and Sunset Strip, this serene hotel has a garden and pool area and provides a welcome escape from the hustle and bustle of the city. Ideally located for shopping and dining. ✆ Map K4 • 469 North Doheny Dr, Beverly Hills • 310-274-8141 • $$$ • www.hotelbeverlyterrace.com

7 Cal Mar Hotel Suites

The flowery bedspreads and sofas may be stuck in the 1980s, but you get an entire apartment for less money than a standard double anywhere else. Units face a landscaped pool. Located in a quiet residential street, Cal Mar is close to Santa Monica hip zones. Free parking. ✆ Map A3 • 220 California Ave • 310-395-5555 • No dis. access • No air conditioning • $$$ • www.calmarhotel.com

8 Loews Santa Monica Beach Hotel

Very close to the sand and Santa Monica Pier, this large resort makes children feel comfortable with activities, special welcome kits, and free stays for those under 18. ✆ Map A4 • 1700 Ocean Ave • 310-458-6700 • $$$$ • www.santamonicaloewshotel.com

9 Disney's Grand Californian Hotel

The price tag is a bit steep at this 751-room resort designed in richly wooded Craftsman style, but standard rooms sleep up to two adults and four kids, and there's even a private entrance to Disney's California Adventure™. ✆ Map G5 • 1600 S Disneyland Dr • 714-956-6425 • $$$$$ • www.disneyland.com

10 Portofino Inn & Suites

This spacious hotel is great for wallet-watchers. The little ones will love camping out in bunk beds and a sofa sleeper and will get their own amenities such as TV, microwave, and fridge as well. ✆ Map D3 • 1831 S Harbor Blvd • 714-782-7600 • $$ • www.portofinoinnanaheim.com

Left **Hilton Checkers Hotel** Center & Right **Loews Hollywood Hotel**

TOP 10 Business Hotels

1 Westin Bonaventure Hotel

With about 20 eateries, pool, fitness club, shops, and a full business center, the landmark Bonaventure has more facilities than most small towns. Regular rooms are smallish, but the office suites are well equipped. ⌾ Map U4 • 404 S Figueroa St • 866-716-8132 • $$$ • www.thebonaventure.com

2 Hilton Checkers Hotel

An island of old-world sophistication in the fast-paced Financial District, this 1929 hotel is great for conducting business in style. Prepare for your meetings in lovely leather chairs at a marble desk. ⌾ Map U5 • 535 S Grand Ave • 213-624-0000 • $$$ • www3.hilton.com

3 Omni Los Angeles Hotel at California Plaza

Walk to Walt Disney Concert Hall, MOCA, and other Downtown landmarks from this modern hotel in the Financial District. Business rooms have huge desks, office equipment, and supplies. ⌾ Map V4 • 251 S Olive St • 213-617-3300 • $$$$ • www.omnihotels.com

4 DoubleTree by Hilton Hotel Los Angeles Downtown

This serene Little Tokyo hotel offers an exotic experience, especially if staying in the Japanese rooms where you sleep on *tatami* mats. The spa and the beautiful third-floor Japanese gardens are great for winding down. ⌾ Map W4 • 120 S Los Angeles St • 213-629-1200 • $$ • http://doubletree3.hilton.com

5 Loews Hollywood Hotel

This art-filled high-rise overlooks Hollywood and Highland. Suites accommodate small meetings. An equipped business center, PC rentals, and secretarial services are also on offer. ⌾ Map P2 • 1755 N Highland Ave • 323-856-1200 • $$$$ • www.loewshotels.com/Hollywood-Hotel

6 Orlando Hotel

Suitable for smaller gatherings, the trump card of this European-style hotel is its location close to the shopping and nightlife in West Hollywood and Beverly Hills. Rates include a daily taxi voucher. ⌾ Map M5 • 8384 W 3rd St • 323-658-6600 • $$$$ • www.theorlando.com

7 SLS Hotel at Beverly Hills

Friendly and efficient staff, a business center with high-speed Internet access, and meeting rooms with assets such as teleconferencing and video equipment are just some of the great perks. ⌾ Map L5 • 465 S La Cienega Blvd • 310-247-0400 • $$$$$ • www.slshotels.com/beverlyhills

8 Luxe Hotel Sunset Boulevard

A lovely property with lush landscaping, this is conveniently located right next to Freeway 405. Spacious rooms in soothing colors feature extras such as DSL and fax machines. ⌾ Map C2 • 11461 Sunset Blvd • 310-476-6571 • $$$$ • www.luxesunset.com

9 Hyatt Regency Century Plaza

This hotel next to Beverly Hills hosts major events, from political fundraisers to pharmaceutical conferences. An overhaul spruced up the pool area and the rooms and added an Asian-inspired spa. ⌾ Map C2 • 2025 Ave of the Stars • 310-228-1234 • $$$$ • www.centuryplaza.hyatt.com

10 Los Angeles Airport Marriott

Close to LAX, this chain hotel is great for business travelers. With just over 1,000 rooms, it has a full range of conference facilities, with business and secretarial services. All rooms have wireless Internet access and high-speed connection is available at an extra cost. ⌾ Map C4 • 5855 W Century Blvd • 310-641-5700 • $$$ • www.marriott.com

Unless otherwise stated, all hotels accept credit cards, have private bathrooms and air conditioning, and provide disabled access

Price Categories

For the cheapest standard double room per night (without breakfast), taxes, and extra charges.

$	under $100
$$	$100–$150
$$$	$150–$250
$$$$	$250–$350
$$$$$	over $350

Left **Venice Beach House** Right **Elaine's Hollywood Bed & Breakfast**

🔟 B&Bs

1 Venice Beach House

Built in 1911 by relatives of Venice founder Abbot Kinney *(see p118)*, this delightful inn is a witness to Venice history. A quiet oasis, it allows you to retreat to the comforts of cozy, antique-filled rooms after a busy day at the beach or in town. 🏠 Map A6 • 15 30th Ave • 310-823-1966 • $$$ • www.venicebeachhouse.com

2 Malibu Bella Vista

Nestled in Malibu Canyon, the ranch-style Bella Vista is ideally located just minutes from the beach and good hiking trails. Spa facilities are available and the excellent Saddle Peak Lodge gourmet restaurant is down the street. 🏠 Map A2 • 25786 Piuma Rd • 818-591-9255 • $ • No dis. access • www.malibubellavista.com

3 Channel Road Inn

A Neo-Colonial home built in 1915, it is clad in wooden shingles and sits on the northern edge of Santa Monica. Each room has different perks such as fireplaces, lovely four-poster beds, patios, soaking tubs, or a view. 🏠 Map B3 • 219 W Channel Rd • 310-459-1920 • $$$ • www.channelroadinn.com

4 Hollywood Bed & Breakfast

Located in a residential area, this quiet, six-room property has a private screening room, parlor, dining room, pool, kitchen, and dance/exercise room, to go with the traditionally-decorated rooms. Free parking and WiFi. 🏠 Map N2 • 1701 N Orange Grove Ave • 323-874-8017 • $$$ • www.hollywoodbandb.com

5 Bissell House

This stately 1887 Victorian home has a prestigious address on Pasadena's "Millionaire's Row." A sedate, grown-up atmosphere reigns in the elegant public areas and all the eight cosy guest rooms. 🏠 Map F2 • 201 Orange Grove Ave • 626-441-3535 • No dis. access • $$$ • www.bissellhouse.com

6 The Secret Garden

Just steps from Sunset Strip, each of the five rooms of this Spanish-Mediterranean home is unique. The hosts whip up amazing breakfasts. 🏠 Map M2 • 8039 Selma Ave • 323-656-3888 • Dis. access in one room • Air conditioning is limited • $$ • www.secretgardenbnb.com

7 Inn at Playa del Rey

A modern breezy B&B, close to the ocean and adjacent to a nature preserve, it is perfect for those who want the convenience of staying near the airport. 🏠 Map C4 • 435 Culver Blvd • 310-574-1920 • $$$ • www.innatplayadelrey.com

8 Inn on Mt. Ada

Live it up in the grandeur of William Wrigley's former hilltop mansion on Catalina Island. Standard rates include breakfast, a light lunch, evening champagne reception, and the use of a golf car so that you can tool around town. 🏠 398 Wrigley Rd • 310-510-2030 • No dis. access • No air conditioning • $$$$$ • www.innonmtada.com

9 Dockside Boat & Bed

A unique getaway, this floating B&B has on offer a fully equipped sailboat, motor yacht, or even a Chinese junk. Boats are moored in Long Beach's Rainbow Harbor; enjoy sunset views of the Queen Mary. 🏠 Map E6 • 316 E Shoreline Dr • 562-436-3111 • No dis. access • Limited air conditioning • $$$ • www.boatandbed.com

10 Elaine's Hollywood Bed & Breakfast

This beautifully restored 1910 bungalow has two rooms available and is located in a quiet neighborhood. Elaine's is a perfect base for exploring Hollywood and West Hollywood and its gracious hosts will help you plan your outings. 🏠 Map N2 • 1616 N Sierra Bonita • 323-850-0766 • $ • No dis. access • No credit cards • www.elaineshollywoodbedandbreakfast.com

➤ *All B&Bs include breakfast as part of room charges*

General Index

Acknowledgments

The Author

Catherine Gerber has observed and documented the evolution of Los Angeles in word and image for nearly 20 years. She remains fascinated by her adopted home's ability to continuously and unapologetically reinvent itself. Her work has appeared in books, newspapers, and magazines in USA and Europe.

Photographer

David Peevers

Additional Photography

Max Alexander, Steve Gorton, Dave King, Susanna Price, Neil Setchfield

AT DK INDIA:
Managing Editor
Aruna Ghose

Art Editor
Benu Joshi

Project Editor
Kajori Aikat

Project Designer
Priyanka Thakur

Senior Cartographer
Uma Bhattacharya

Cartographer
Suresh Kumar

Picture Researcher
Taiyaba Khatoon

Fact Checker
Janet Grey, Aimee Lind

Indexer & Proofreader
Bhavna Sharma

DTP Co-ordinator
Shailesh Sharma

DTP Designer
Vinod Harish

AT DK LONDON:
Publisher
Douglas Amrine

Publishing Manager
Jane Ewart

Senior Cartographic Editor
Casper Morris

Senior DTP Designer
Jason Little

Picture Research
Brigitte Arora, Rachel Barber, Marta Bescos, Rhiannon Furbear, Ellen Root

Production
Shane Higgins

Revisions Team
Rhiannon Furbear, Claire Jones, Bharti Karakoti, Sumita Khatwani, Priyanka Kumar, Alison McGill, Carolyn Patten, Rada Radojicic, Susana Smith, Ajay Verma, Sylvia Tombesi-Walton, Hugo Wilkinson

Picture Credits
Key:
a-above; b-below/bottom; c-centre; f-far; l-left; r-right; t-top.

This Book makes reference to various Disney copyrighted characters, trademarks, marks, and registered marks owned by The Walt Disney Company and Disney Enterprises, Inc. The publishers would like to thank Disney Enterprises Inc. for their kind permission to reproduce the photographs: 7clb, 30cla, 30-31c, 30bc, 31bl, 32tl, 32tr, 32b, 33t, 34t, 34br, 35cl, 35b and Petersen Automotive Museum: 102tr

Works of art have been reproduced with the permission of the following copyright holders: *Untitled Improvisation III*, 1914 Vasily Kandinsky ©ADAGP, Paris and DACS, London 2007

18tc; *Ceci n'est pas une pipe*, 1928 René Magritte ©ADAGP, Paris and DACS, London 2007 16cla.

The publishers would also like to thank the following individuals, companies, and picture libraries for their kind permission to reproduce their photographs.

ACESTOCK LTD., London: Steve Goddard 56bc, 97tr; AVALON HOLLYWOOD: 60cl.

THE BUNNY MUSEUM: 62tl.

CHAYA RESTAURANTS & CMC ASSOCIATES, INC., LLC: 109tl; COLE'S: 79tl; CORBIS: 3tl, 136tl, 142tr; Hal Beral 36crb; Yann Arthus-Bertrand 7crb, 28-29c, 102cl; Bettmann 35cl, 35b, 38tl, 139t; Kevin Burke 120-121; Dean Conger 30-31c, 30bc; Richard Cummins 19bl; Macduff Everton 32b, 33t, 34t; Robert Holmes 30cla, 39r; Dave G. Houser 94 cr; Dewitt Jones 28br; Robert Landau 6cla, 11bc, 22ca, 22br, 34br, 65tr, 86tl, 92tl, 98-99; Richard T. Nowitz 57tr; Roger Ressmeyer 127t; Bill Ross 1c; Joseph Sohm; ChromoSohm Inc. 68-69; Douglas Slone 6clb; Frank Trapper 59tr; Peter Turnley 38tr; Nik Wheeler 8cb, 32tl, 113tl, 132-133, 135tl; Alison Wright 31bl; CORBIS SABA: David Butow 100tl; CORBIS SYGMA: Koester Axel 96b.

DREAMSTIME.COM: Merkuri2 58tl.

EL REY THEATRE: 60tr; ELAINE'S HOLLYWOOD B&B: 151tc.

GETTY IMAGES: AFP/Robyn Beck 60tl; Michael Buckner 60tr; © J PAUL GETTY TRUST: 12cla; *Irises* by

Vincent van Gogh, Dutch, Saint-Rémy, France, 1889 Oil on Canvas 28 x 36-5/8 in. 90.PA.20 12-13c, *Wheatstacks, Snow Effect Morning* by Claude Monet, French, Giverny, 1891 Oil on Canvas 25-1/2 x 39-1/4 in. 95.PA.63 12br, *Modern Rome - Campo Vaccino* by JMW Turner, British, 1839 oil on canvas 36 1/8 x 48 1/4 in. 2011.6 13tl, *Cabinet on Stand* Attributed to André-Charles Boulle, ébéniste; and Jean Varin, medalist, French, Paris, about 1678-1680 H: 7ft. 6-1/2 in.; W: 4ft. 11-1/2 in.; D: 2ft. 2-1/4 in. 77.DA.1, *Abduction by Europa* by Rembrandt Harmensz. van Rijn, Dutch, 1632 Oil on Panel 24-1/2 x 30-5/16 in. 95. PB.7; GRANGER COLLECTION, NEW YORK: 38bl.

© THE HUNTINGTON LIBRARY, ART COLLECTIONS, & BOTANICAL GARDENS: 7tr, 22-23c, 23tl, 23clb, 24tl, 24tc, 24tr, 24bc; INDEX STOCK IMAGERY: Mick Roessler 74–75; LATHER INC.: 92tr; LACONVENTION & VISITORS' BUREAU: Michele & Tom Grimme 137tr. © LOEWS HOLLYWOOD HOTEL: 150tc, 150tr.

© 2007 MUSEUM ASSOC-IATES /LOS ANGELES COUNTY MUSEUM OF ART: *La Trahison des Images (Ceci n'est pas une pipe)* by René Magritte, purchased with funds provided by the Mr. and Mrs. William Preston Harrison Collection 16cla, *Padmasambhava (Guru Ripoche)* Gift of the James and Paula Coburn Foundation 17clb; *Mother about to Wash Her Sleepy Child* by Mary Cassatt, 1880 Oil on canvas, Mrs. Fred Hathaway Bixby Bequest 16cb, *In the Woods at Giverny: Blanch Hoschedé at Her Easel with Suzanne Hoschedé* by Claude Monet, 1887 Oil on canvas, Mr. and Mrs. George Gard De Sylva Collection 17tr, *Untitled Improvisation III* by Vasily Kandinsky, 1914, Oil on card-board, Museum acquisition by exchange from David E. Bright Bequest 18tc, *The Magdalen with the Smoking Flame* by Georges de La Tour, c. 1638-40, Oil on canvas, gift of The Ahmanson Foundation 18tr, *Standing Warrior*, West El Arenal Brown style, Mexico, Jalisco, ca. 200 B.C. – A.D. 400, Ceramic with burnished red slip and painted black and cream decoration, The Proctor Stafford Collection, purchased with funds provided by Mr. and Mrs. Allan C. Balch MASTER- FILE: Gail Mooney 4–5. © 2003 THE NORTON SIMON FOUNDATION: *Still Life with Lemons, Oranges and a Rose* by Francisco de Zurbarán, Spanish, 1633, Oil on canvas 24-1/2 x 43-1/8 in. F.1972.06.P 42tr, *Self-Portrait* by Rembrandt van Rijn, c.1636-38, Dutch, Oil on panel 24-7/8 x 19-3/4 in. F.1969.18.P 90tc, *Exotic Landscape* by Henri Rousseau, French,1910, Oil on canvas 51-1/4 x 64 in. F.1971.3.P 90tr.

THE PALEY CENTER FOR MEDIA:110tl.

SMART DESTINATIONS INC: 140tl; SUNSET ENTERTAINMENT GROUP: 101tl.

© UNIVERSAL STUDIOS HOLLYWOOD: 27clb; Shrek 4-D 26tr. VALENTINO RESTAURANT: 28tr; VFM LEONARDO INC.: 144tr.

© 2003 UNIVERSAL STUDIOS INC.: 7cra, 28tr, 26-27c, 27tl, 27bc.

All other images are © Dorling Kindersley. For further information see *www.dkimages.com*.